Young Writers was
been passionately ι
reading and writing
ever since. The que   .,. roung
Writers remains as cc   .-ᴜ ιo engendering the
fostering of burgeoning poetic and literary talent as
ever.

This year's Young Writers competition has proven
as vibrant and dynamic as ever and we are
delighted to present a showcase of the best poetry
from across the UK. Each poem has been carefully
selected from a wealth of *Once Upon A Rhyme*
entries before ultimately being published in this, our
twelfth primary school poetry series.

Once again, we have been supremely impressed by
the overall high quality of the entries we have
received. The imagination, energy and creativity
which has gone into each young writer's entry made
choosing the best poems a challenging and often
difficult but ultimately hugely rewarding task - the
general high standard of the work submitted amply
vindicating this opportunity to bring their poetry to a
larger appreciative audience.

We sincerely hope you are pleased with our final
selection and that you will enjoy *Once Upon A
Rhyme Lancashire* for many years to come.

Young Writers
2004 POETRY COMPETITION

ONCE UPON A RHYME

IMAGINATION FOR
A NEW GENERATION

Lancashire
Edited Steve Twelvetree

 Young**Writers**
First published in Great Britain in 2004 by:
Young Writers
Remus House
Coltsfoot Drive
Peterborough
PE2 9JX
Telephone: 01733 890066
Website: www.youngwriters.co.uk

SB ISBN 1 84460 509 4

Contents

Ruby Wilson (9)	21
Abigail Stroud-Mort (9)	22
Joshua Riley (9)	23

Eccleston Primary School

Nicola Moss (8)	23
Richard Hopkinson (8)	24
Danielle Hilton (9)	24
Alex Weetman (9)	25
Daniel Eccles (8)	25
Michael Bleasdale (8)	26
Chloe Miller (8)	26
Ellie Forrest (8)	27
Calvin Merry (8)	27
Alex Bennett-Forshaw (9)	28
Rebecca Bradley (8)	28
Alice Davies (8)	29
Kyle Hesketh (9)	29
Ryan Banks (9)	30
James Frankland (8)	30
Lisa Quickfall (8)	31
Craig Everton (9)	31
Matthew Thompson (8)	32

Greenhill Primary School

Rachael Worrall (10)	32
Charlotte Snell (11)	33
Matthew Brock (11)	33
Lauren Farrow (9)	34
Joshua Rowlands (11)	34
Amy Quigley (9)	35
Mark Dean (10)	35
Sarah Kidd (9)	36
Rebecca Pollard (10)	36
Saffron Emily Burgess (7)	37
Robert Bromley (11)	37
Ryan Holmes (9)	38
Haydn Brown (10)	38
Georgia Whittles (9)	38
Lauren Madden (10)	39
Kate Allanson (10)	39

Habib Shama (9)	39
Amy Dunn (9) & Jennifer Naisbett (8)	40
Rachael Lytham (9)	40
Esther Morrissey (8)	40
Caitlin Cole (8)	41
Hannah Simons (8)	41
Hannah Worrall (7)	41
Emily Fuller (8)	42
Elizabeth Alblas (7)	42
Jenny Keen (9)	43
Megan Giffard (7)	43
Matthew Brown (7)	44
Alexandra Rose White (7)	44
Anna Tollitt (7)	44
Ruth Merrick (10)	45
Sarah Pollard (7)	45
Charlotte Dunkley (8)	45
Reece Spencer (9)	46
Rebecca Carr (10)	46
Tomas Helliwell (9)	46
Danni Critchley (11)	47
Samantha Spencer (9)	47
Jacob Eardley-Dutton (9)	47
Sophie Stone Smith (8)	48
Chloe Walker (10)	48
Carly Lockey (11)	48
Amy Smith (9)	49
Rachel Reay (9)	49

Hawthorns Junior School

Mohmed Valibhai (8)	50
Muhammad Chopdat (8)	50
Sonia Khalid (8)	50
Zenab Hussain (10)	51
Shabnam Rehman (8)	51
Ikra Hassain (8)	51
Sheikl Iqbal (11)	52
Adil Hussain (10)	52
Humaira Khan (8)	52
Muneeba Khalil (7)	53
Obeid Soge (8)	53

Razee Khaliq (10)	53
Zulkernain Hussain (10)	54
Abdul Gaffar Aslam (11)	54
Akmal Ali (9)	54
Zubare Sidik (10)	55
Tayyib Hussain (8)	55
Taniya Hussain (9)	55
Faheema Mehboob Adam (10)	56
Mariya Shaikh (11)	57
Junaid Asghar (9)	57
Shamim Chopdat (11)	58
Aqib Butt (11)	58
Ebrahim Chand (11)	59
Sundus Siddiqui (11)	59
Kushof Hussain (7)	59
Kulsum Hussain (9)	60

Holden Clough Primary School

Oliver Tomlinson (8)	60
Imran Sheikh (8)	60
Megan White	61
Daniel Lanham (8)	61
Ravina Jobanputra (8)	61
Samuel Fleetwood Myles (7)	62
Benjamin Peter Coleman (8)	62
Ayesha Ul-haq (9)	63
Matthew Taylor (8)	63
Anna Elizabeth Davies (9)	64
Hannah Margaret Millin (8)	64
Sarah Mellor (8)	65
Emma Walton (9)	65
Dina Mardania (8)	66
Rachel Halliday (7)	66
Georgia Main (9)	67
Clarice Jean Lee-Alker (9)	67
George Dalton (9)	68
Naomi Fletcher (8)	68
Chloe Louise Wyatt (9)	69
Nikita Patel (8)	69
Samuel Wellfair (7)	70
Aidan Quinn (8)	70

Matthew Halliday (10)	71
Alexander James Spencer (9)	71
Joshua Nolan (11)	72
Hamaad Yousaf (8)	72
Charlotte Louise Young (11)	73
Jessica Dyson (8)	73
Archana Chauhan (8)	74
Emily Bleackley (8)	74
Kathryn Booth (11)	74
Yasmin Etches (9)	75
Stephen Crane (9)	75
Luke Hirst (8)	75
Richard Selby (11)	76
Charlotte Vaughan (10)	77
Divya Khilosia (11)	78
Ben Bowker (8)	78
Sejal Dhorajiwala (11)	79
Joseph Slifkin (8)	79
Amman Khan (11)	80
Joshua Ramiah (10)	80
Matthew David Lewis (11)	81
Rebekah Choudhury (10)	81
Jake Forrest (10)	82
Mohammed Zubair Khan (11)	82
Jack Mather (11)	83
Taybah Gufar (8)	83
Neha Ahmed (8)	84

Holy Infant & St Anthony School

Amanda Wood (11)	84
Lauren McKee (10)	85
Matthew Jeffs (10)	85
Hayley Walton (10)	86
Jane O'Rourke (10)	87
Stacey Gray (11)	88
Holly Howarth (9)	88
Megan Andrews (9)	89
Naomi Sarsfield (10)	89
Amber Mayo (9)	90
Molly Johnson (10)	90
Nicole Jones (10)	91

Joseph Harrison (10)   91
Harriet Killeen (10)   92

Ightcnlilll Primary School
Daniel Groves (9)   92
Louisa Burrows (9)   93
Abigail Bowling (8)   93
Sarah Bushby (8)   93
Lydia Fairclough (9)   94
Charlotte Sanders (8)   94
Heather Clements (8)   95
Jack Heyworth (8)   95
Stephen Rostron (8)   96
Chloe Colton (9)   96
Adele Morrell (8)   97
Jack Green (9)   97
Lucy Victoria Davis (9)   98

Nether Kellet Community Primary School
Luke Stephenson (8)   98
Danielle Simpson (7)   98
Danielle Watts (9)   99
Lydia Cowell (7)   99
Elanor Brown (9)   100

Our Lady & St Hubert's RC Primary School
Joseph Birtwell (11)   100
Oliver Woodall (9)   101
Bethany Hargreaves (11)   101
Jessica Coy (11)   102
Charleigh Dunn (10)   102
Hannah Parker (11)   103
Dominic Hogan (11)   103
Hannah Sharkey (10)   104
Linden Smith (10)   104
Charlotte Mulcahy (11)   105
Kane Moreton (10)   106
Sam Hoole (10)   106
Tobin Joseph (9)   106
John Parker (10)   107

Natalie Walker (11)	124
Shannon Booth (10)	125
Ben Howarth (11)	126
Steven Taylor (10)	126
Iqra Mahmood (10)	127
Sam Fitzpatrick (10)	127
Natasha Tyrie (10)	128
Abigail Kitchen (11)	128
Jake Dolsey (11)	129

St Thomas' CE Primary School, Lytham St Annes

James Cummings (8)	129
Liam Bloor (7)	130

St Thomas' CE Primary School, Barrowford

Sarah Gillard (10)	130
Becky Nolan (10)	131
Helena Chadwick (9)	131
Daisy Stinchon (10)	132
Ruth Hallows (10)	132
Samantha Caraher (10)	132
Kate Webster (9)	133

The Valley Community School

Ammaarah Patel (10)	133
Bilal Patel (11)	134
Ashraf Patel (11)	134
Irfan Patel (10)	134
Weseema Patel (11)	135
Aameena Mohammed (10)	135
Raees Patel (11)	135
Naushaad Patel (10)	136
Nasira Patel (11)	136
Mohamed Bhaiji (11)	137
Suhail Mahomed (11)	137
Amin Adam (10)	138
Shajeda Sidda (11)	138
Asifali Adam (10)	138
Aysha Bhaloda (11)	139

Thorn CP School
Lauren Downes	139
Abbey Broadbent (6)	140
Jessica Procter (7)	140
Kayleigh McGuinness (11)	141

Westholme Middle School
Cynthia Li (11)	141
David Lee (8)	142
Rebecca Arton (11)	142
Sophie Janus (10)	143
Ruby Kay (10)	143
Hannah MacIntosh (10)	144
Megan Hindle (10)	145
Harriet Salvesen-Sawh (9)	146
Emily Green (11)	146
Rachael Moodie (10)	147
Fiona Blacklidge (11)	147
Romana Alli (10)	148
Simone Masterson (9) & Emma Louise Booth (10)	149
Rosie McCann (10)	150
Jack Bolton (7)	150
Tori Redmond (10)	151
Emily Earnshaw (10)	151
Vicky Haworth (10)	152
Matthew Parker (7)	152
Alice Singleton (10)	153
Lucy Shephard (11)	153

Whittle-Le-Woods Primary School
Patrick McMullan (8)	154
Shannon Touhey (8)	154
Keira Skillen (8)	154
Hannah Vickerman (8)	155
Lily Dickinson (8)	155
Sarah Hanrahan (8)	155
Shannen Jo Lupton (10)	156
Aneesh Bhadra (9)	156
Emily Toplis (10)	157
Jennifer Litwinski (11)	157
Grace Pulsford (10)	158

Rachel Hull (10)   158
George Dobson (10)   159
Ryan Downs (10)   159
Lucy Griffiths (10)   160
Jessica Hall (10)   161
Thomas Robinson (10)   162
Sarah Knowles (10)   162
Aaron Morris (10)   162
Alexandra Rae Rimmer (11)   163
James McIver (10)   163
Jordan Heyworth (10)   163
Sophie Smith (11)   164
James McGovern (11)   164
Bethan Swanwick (10)   165
Samuel Pattison (11)   165

XII Apostles RC Primary School
Ashley Brown (10)   166
Andrew Hodson (10)   166
Louise McDonald (10)   166
Priscilla Devine (10)   167
Jonathan Sephton (11)   167
Thomas Rudd (11)   167
Ben Turner (11)   168
Nicole Fasoli (11)   168
Kelly Causby (10)   168
Naomi Green (11)   169
Thomas Spencer (10)   169
Margaret Unsworth (11)   169
Curtis Barnett (10)   170
Victoria Carney (11)   170
Jonathan Ogden (11)   170
Lauren Nicholas (10)   171
Aiden Slack (11)   171

The Poems

Weather

There are many weather types
Some making a loud noise
There's wind and rain, snow and hail
There's thunder and lightning and sometimes a gale.

The sun makes me feel really glad
The rain is really terrible
When it's sunny I can play
When it's rainy I have to do my homework.

The snow is really fun
The hail hits you quite hard
The snowflakes are in different shapes
The hail's just like a big ice ball.

Lightning is very nice to see
Thunder makes a really loud noise
But it can make a fire
And it can make a real mess.

So you see some can be very dangerous
But some can be excellent
I prefer the sun
But the rain, absolutely awful.

Jack Wilkinson (11)
Arkholme CE Primary School

Sounds

I like the sound of the bird's little call,
I like the sound of the bird's little call,
I like the sound of the echo in the hall.
I like the sound of the rustling trees,
I like the sound of the humming bees.
The sound of the water running down the creek.
The sound of the rain is beautiful too,
But the worst sound of all is the moo,
Just when a cow has milked.

Grace Cousins (9)
Arkholme CE Primary School

The Storm

The wind is howling like a wolf
A dog is growling in the wood.
The lightning flashes, lighting up the sky,
The thunder clashes, how worried am I?

I think there's a storm, I'm really scared.
I want just to cuddle up in bed,
And hide my head.
Mummy and Daddy are both asleep,
Brother and Sister dare not peep.
But I am awake shivering here in the cold,
Trying my hardest to be very bold.

Kirsty Abraham (10)
Arkholme CE Primary School

Death

Death is a feeling that creeps up behind you.
The colour of death is jet-black.
The smell of death is burnt toast.
Death looks like a ghost-stricken forest.
In the end Death just takes you away where
You can't enjoy all the fun, all the parties,
All the weekends, or most of all, your family.
Death just takes it away . . .
Death just takes it away . . .
Death just takes it away!

Joshua Thomas (9)
Arkholme CE Primary School

My Mum

My mum wears a bright pink wig,
And her laugh sounds like a pig.
All my friends think she's strange,
And totally out of range.
Sometimes I do agree,
She's totally different to me,
She really is embarrassing,
Especially when she starts to sing!

Nicola Benson (10)
Arkholme CE Primary School

Jealousy

Jealousy is green with envy,
It smells like a banquet you can't reach.
It tastes like a mediocre meal,
Jealousy sound like an unfair music competition.
It feels like being
Pushed backward by the wind.
Jealousy lives in even the smallest of us.

Ben Hall (11)
Arkholme CE Primary School

Snail Poem

Once I saw a snail, crawling up the wall.
I saw him in my bedroom, and then in the school hall.
He crawled on a chair, and he was very small.
He left a trail behind him, then curled up in a ball.

Jake Howard (10)
Chantlers Primary School

The Journey

An early morning after dawn,
A young girl stepped on a bus,
She struggled through right to the back,
Away from noise and fuss.

A man was stood in front of her,
He wouldn't let her pass;
She spoke quite politely,
But he shoved her against the glass.

He started saying rude remarks,
Some words she did not know.
He told her to go back
To where she came from, 'Go!'

She went to school filled
With puzzlement and awe;
But later in life she understood.
What she had heard and saw.

Racism shouldn't happen
We're all the same inside;
It just makes people feel bad,
Wanting to run and to hide.

Charlotte Edwards (11)
Chantlers Primary School

One Monday Morning

In the quiet world of my surroundings,
I stood there in the cold.
I felt the pain rush through my heart,
No friendship to behold.

I looked up in sadness,
And saw them laugh at me.
Their eyes were used as daggers,
As they walked all over me.

Kicking, punching at my face,
I couldn't take any more;
I looked at my body head to toe,
They'd ripped me to the core.

They walked away feeling happy,
And I turned away in fear.
I felt my body cry out in sorrow,
As I slowly shed a tear.

I am now a happy 26-year-old,
Jolly as can be.
So please don't let them get you down,
Like they did to me.

Katherine Wilson (11)
Chantlers Primary School

Upset After School

One day after school,
I was at the bus stop.
The bus slowed down,
And a man told me to stop.

'Go back to where you came from.'
Is what he said to me,
I didn't know what he meant,
That's what I was doing, didn't he see?

I didn't know what he was talking about,
But got on the bus, hurt and confused.
I sat near the window side,
Wondering why, totally bemused.

I started to feel very worried;
What if they do it again?
I felt lonely, all alone;
Closing my eyes against the pain.

Hannah Jones (10)
Chantlers Primary School

All About Ebony

I have a little fluffy rabbit, that I called Ebony,
She is so very cuddly when I sit her on my knee.
I love her so very much,
And Dad has made her a two-storey hutch.

I feed her each day, with carrots and hay,
As she runs round and plays
Her little nose twitches
It's so much fun she has me in stitches.

Chloe Tomson (9)
Chantlers Primary School

Lee Lane

Suzie looked out the window;
On to the beckoning Lee Lane.
They were waiting to call,
It would start all over again.

She stepped out of the door, scared, confused;
Why me? Why can't I be right?
The gang turned round the corner,
Suzie suddenly flinched with fright.

'But they're just bullies,'
Her mum said, turning her around,
A tear trickled down Suzie's face,
No justice was found.

Now you know what it's like,
To be teased, scared to go on outings,
So you now can stop it,
Before war, and people shouting!

Laura Magrath (11)
Chantlers Primary School

The Poem Of The Snails

Baby snails are very small,
And also very slimy.
They eat leaves and things like that,
And leave a trail that's shiny.

I like snails big, round and fat,
They go in churches' steeples.
They are played with by children,
And eaten by French people.

Daniel Lewis (9)
Chantlers Primary School

Learn To Get Along

'Look Tom, she is going to cry,
Should I give her a dress tip?
I bet she is wondering why.
Look Tom, look at her lip.'

'I'm only trying to get on the bus,
Listen guys I have had enough.
What would the world be like if we
                        were all the same?
Fighting, in pain.'

'Move out of my way,
Don't lecture us all day.
Listen you go away,
I don't want you lecturing me all day.'

I'm not taking this any longer,
I will lecture you much longer.
I will teach you right,
Forget the wrong,

And learn to get along.'

Samantha Rose (11)
Chantlers Primary School

Kindness

Kindness is watery-blue and white
It smells like strawberry sweets.
Kindness tastes surprisingly like chocolate ice cream,
It sounds like little bluebirds singing happily in the morning,
It feels wonderfully soft like feathers and fur.

Keira Heron (10)
Chantlers Primary School

Autumn

A utumn leaves falling gracefully from trees and hedgehogs
shuffling around the old oak tree picking up acorns and berries.
U nderneath leaves are conkers and helicopters, they're fun
to play with but some not easy to break.
T he conkers grow on chestnut trees and there are no more roses
on the bush.
U mbrellas are always up now and we pick the apples before it
rains again.
M anes on horses are covered up with leaves from head to neck.
N anny is asleep in a rocking chair and outside it is cold with
leaves on the ground.

Erin Jagger (7)
Chantlers Primary School

Hate

Hate is muddy-black and misty-grey,
It smells like dirt and rotten pollution.
Hate tastes burnt and stingingly spicy,
It sounds like nuclear explosions,
Hate feels painfully sharp and rough,
And lives in the deep, black heart of the underworld.

Adam Hargreaves (10)
Chantlers Primary School

Death

Death is black and white like an old dusty television screen,
It feels like slimy like grease from the grill in the kitchen,
It tastes like rotten cakes in an old tin,
It sounds as if someone has broken a piano,
It feels cold and lives at the end of life.

Kieran Cunliffe (9)
Chantlers Primary School

Autumn

A utumn is a wonderful season because you can see
the leaves drifting to the ground.
U nder leaves there can be hedgehogs.
T he squirrels collect different kinds of nuts.
U mbrellas can turn inside out at windy autumn time.
M e and my mum like picking up different types of leaves.
N obody in my family picks up the leaves in the garden.

Alana Grundy (8)
Chantlers Primary School

Endangered

The dolphin is almost extinct, but why?
You sit by the sea and hear them cry,
Boats with fishing nets go by.

They swim in the sea and feel free,
As happy as can be as fishermen catch our tea,
But the dolphin gets caught up too, you see!

Megan Screeton (9)
Chantlers Primary School

Up In The Attic

Up in the attic,
Xmas decs waiting for next December.
Old toys from when my grandpa was a lad.
Books that my mum read when she was young.
Dust that makes me sneeze. 'Achoo!'
Babies' clothes that are too small.
An old Scalextric that is rusty.

Tim Sharples (9)
Eagley Junior School

War

In the cellar down below,
All I hear is bombs that blow.
At least it's safe in the cold and dark,
This war has certainly made its mark.

Children crying
People dying
When will the terror end?

People have gone off to fight,
But who will make all this right?
It isn't fair all this pain,
I hope the bombing doesn't start again.

Children crying
People dying
When will the terror end?

No more water, no more fun,
The soldiers have started to use a gun.
The armies march through the streets,
In the cellar my racing heart beats.

Children crying
People dying
When will the terror end?

When my mum's friend died,
Everybody cried and cried.
Children have no parents now,
I would help but I don't know how.

Children crying
People dying
When will the terror end?

Some day, somehow
I hope the terror ends!

Josie Garmory (10)
Eagley Junior School

Ten Green Monsters

Ten green monsters standing in a line,
One hurt his spine, then there were nine.

Nine green monsters standing on a plate,
One slipped over, then there were eight.

Eight green monsters went to Devon,
One lost his sun hat, then there were seven.

Seven green monsters eating a Twix,
One got too fat, then there were six.

Six green monsters went in a beehive,
One got stung, then there were five.

Five green monsters standing on the floor,
One slipped on a banana peel, then there were four.

Four green monsters climbed a tree,
One fell off, then there were three.

Three green monsters on the loo,
One fell in, then there were two.

Two green monsters lying in the sun,
One got burned, then there was one.

One green monster eating a bun,
He got poisoned, then there were none.

Owen McCann (10)
Eagley Junior School

Ten White Snowmen

Ten white snowmen standing on the double yellow line,
One had to pay a fine, then there were nine.

Nine white snowmen looking for a mate,
One had a date, then there were eight.

Eight white snowmen going to Devon,
One got car sick, then there were seven.

Seven white snowmen taking some sips,
One got the hiccups, then there were six.

Six white snowmen stranding near a beehive,
One got stung, then there were five.

Five white snowmen standing near a door,
One got knocked over, then there were four.

Four white snowmen standing in the sea,
One's leg cracked, then there were three.

Three white snowmen shouting, 'Boo!'
One got a shock, then there were two.

Two white snowmen meeting Ron,
He cast a spell, then there was one.

One white snowman all alone in the sun
He vanished into the air and then there were none.

Peter Entwistle (10)
Eagley Junior School

Ten White Snowmen

Ten white snowmen standing in a line,
One got hit, then there were nine,

Nine white snowmen putting on some weight,
One got fat, then there were eight.

Eight white snowmen on holiday in Devon,
One drowned in the sea and then there were seven.

Seven white snowmen doing tricks,
One turned into a rabbit, then there were six.

Six white snowmen in a beehive,
One got stung and then there were five.

Five white snowmen went to war,
One got killed, then there were four.

Four white snowmen having a cup of tea,
It was too hot for one, then there were three.

Three white snowmen with nothing much to do,
One got bored and ran away, then there were two.

Two white snowmen set off for a run,
One didn't make it back, then there was one.

One white snowman after there had been so many,
He melted like the others, then there weren't any.

Emma Cunningham (10)
Eagley Junior School

Ten White Snowmen

Ten white snowmen drinking wine,
One got drunk, then there were nine.

Nine white snowmen had to wait,
One melted, then there were eight.

Eight white snowmen sat in Devon,
One was left, then there were seven.

Seven white snowmen playing with bricks,
One got squashed, then there were six.

Six white snowmen eating chives,
One got sick, then there were five.

Five white snowmen running out of power,
Four got powered up, then there were four.

Four white snowmen drinking tea,
One of them got too hot, then there were three.

Three white snowmen playing with goo,
One got covered in it, then there were two.

Two white snowmen eating scones,
One got full up, then there was one.

One white snowman dead and gone,
There are none now, so now there are none.

Daniel Slater (10)
Eagley Junior School

Ten White Snowmen

Ten white snowmen fell into a mine,
One went too far and then there were nine.

Nine white snowmen eating off a plate,
One got food poisoning and then there were eight.

Eight white snowmen went to Heaven,
One died there and then there were seven.

Seven white snowmen, one found a brick,
He picked it up and chucked it and then there were six.

Six white snowmen, one had a wife,
One was haunted and then there were five.

Five white snowmen went on tour,
One got lost and then there were four.

Four white snowmen had a cup of tea,
One got poisoned and then there were three.

Three white snowmen, one was on the loo,
He fell in and then there were two.

Two white snowmen were messing with guns,
One got shot and then there was one.

One white snowman all alone,
He got lonely and then there were none.

Marc Stapleton (9)
Eagley Junior School

Ten White Snowmen

Ten white snowmen committing a crime,
One got caught and then there were nine.

Nine white snowmen putting on weight,
One got too fat and then there were eight.

Eight white snowmen met a guy called Kevin,
One went off with him and then there were seven.

Seven white snowmen starting to tick,
One got confused and then there were six.

Six white snowmen in a beehive,
One got stung and then there were five.

Five white snowmen went to war,
One got killed and then there were four.

Four white snowmen eating their tea,
One got poisoned and then there were three.

Three white snowmen shouting, 'Boo!'
One lost his voice and then there were two.

Two white snowmen having a run,
One got tired and then there was one.

One white snowman eating a bun,
Then he melted and then there were none!

George Coleman (9)
Eagley Junior School

A Fright In The Night

Poised at the top of the stairway at night,
From the sounds below it could be a fight,
With her thin, chilly fingers curled in fear,
She stealthily walked downstairs to have a peer,
She got to the bottom feeling braver than before,
Then walked over to the living room door.

Suddenly someone grabbed her hip,
So she had to find something to grip,
She found the light switch then turned on the light,
But when it was on she got a fright,
Because someone was in her house at night.

She looked around to see who was there,
She saw someone and started to stare,
Her only daughter had come to make her meal,
How silly that made her feel,
And this is what her daughter said,
'It's OK Mum, you can go back to bed!'

Chloe Johnston (9)
Eagley Junior School

Food Yummy, Yummy

I like food,
It's really yummy,
Once I had a chocolate bunny.

I like food,
It's really tasty,
I like the shortcrust pastry.

I like food
My mum makes,
Because she bakes delicious fairy cakes.

This is my poem about food,
Il hope I'll write more soon.

Rebecca Hailwood (10)
Eagley Junior School

My Family

My family is just plain smart,
But they aren't really good at art.
They make stories all the time,
And have to have a glass of wine.
That's just my family.

At school my sister's top of the class,
And my dad always lets out gas.
Mum works in a sweet shop down the street,
And my brother has a mate called Pete.
That's just my family.

My dog is crazy,
But really lazy.
I have a fish called Lips,
Once it gave me a couple of tips.
That's just my family.

My uncle is always drunk,
And my cousin's a punk.
My grandma's into rock 'n' roll,
My grandad's always collecting bowls.
That's just my crazy family.

Danielle Marriott (10)
Eagley Junior School

Pleasure Beach Fun

Going through the door
And getting your wrist band
Means it's time to have fun.
Turning up and down
And shaking side to side
Makes you feel dizzy and wobbly.
Winning toys and making noise
You feel like a different person.
Jester shows and hey who knows
You might come back next month.

Veronica Finney (10)
Eagley Junior School

Ten White Snowmen

Ten while snowmen all drinking wine,
One got drunk, then there were nine.

Nine white snowmen all got a date,
One got dumped and then there were eight.

Eight white snowmen all went to Heaven,
One had a fight, then there were seven.

Seven white snowmen all snapping sticks,
One got kicked, then there were six.

Six white snowmen all in a drive,
One got knocked over, then there were five.

Five white snowmen all breaking the law,
One got caught, then there were four.

Four white snowmen standing by the River Dee,
One fell in, then there were three.

Three white snowmen playing peek-a-boo,
One got a shock, then there were two.

Two white snowmen all having a run,
One got exhausted, then there was one.

One white snowman standing alone,
The sun melted him, then there were none.

Jade Whalley (10)
Eagley Junior School

Ten White Snowmen

Ten white snowmen under a vine,
One got caught, then there were nine.

Nine white snowmen standing up straight,
One ripped up, then there were eight.

Eight white snowmen went to Devon,
One went to Heaven, then there were seven.

Seven white snowmen playing some tricks,
One disappeared, then there were six.

Six white snowmen drinking near a hive,
One went too close, then there were five.

Five, white snowmen saw a boar,
One went too close, then there were four.

Four white snowmen had some tea,
One got too hot, then there were three.

Three white snowmen went to the zoo,
One got eaten, then there were two.

Two white snowmen in the sun,
One melted, then there was one.

One white snowman was all alone,
He crumbled, then there were none.

Ruby Wilson (9)
Eagley Junior School

Ten White Snowmen

Ten white snowmen drinking some wine,
One got drunk, then there were nine.

Nine white snowmen eating off a plate,
One got too full, then there were eight.

Eight white snowmen they all went to Devon,
One got homesick, then there were seven.

Seven white snowmen, one played tricks,
He made a mistake and then there were six.

Six white snowmen, one took a drive,
He crashed into something, then there were five.

Five white snowmen, one broke his jaw,
He was rushed to hospital, then there were four.

Four white snowmen, one saw a bee,
He then got stung, then there were three.

Three white snowmen, one said, 'Boo!'
The other one got scared, then there were two.

Two white snowmen having some fun,
One got kicked by a football, then there was one.

One white snowman standing on his own,
He started to get lonely, then there were none.

Abigail Stroud-Mort (9)
Eagley Junior School

The Biggest Firework

The biggest firework
Ever lit,
Fizzed, banged,
Glittered and flew.
In gold - silver -
Red - green and blue
It rocketed
So far away
It brought the night
To a burst of day.
Electric bulbs
A million bright
Of shining spray.

But of its magic fiery spell,
All that is left
Is the smoke, the smell.

Joshua Riley (9)
Eagley Junior School

I Am Happy

The sun is shining,
The horses are neighing,
It is a beautiful day.
The flowers are waking,
Dogs are barking
And people are talking,
It is time to play.
Time for me to wake the dog.
Oh a beautiful day to go to the park,
Go to the pond it is so beautiful.
The ducks are quacking,
Baby ones are hatching
From their shells.

Nicola Moss (8)
Eccleston Primary School

With All My Money

With all my money,
I'm going to buy a bunny.
With my skill,
Doh! I forgot to pay the bill.
With my hand,
I can make a rock band.
With my finger,
I can start learning my behaviour.
With my brain,
Yey! I can fix my chain.
With my eye,
I can see people say, 'Goodbye.'
With my lips,
I can taste fish and chips.
With my pen,
I can draw a den.
With my nose
I can smell people's feet and toes.
With my head
I can snuggle in my bed.
With my knees,
I can kill the bees.
With my knuckle,
I can see a chuckle.
With my elbow
I can use a crossbow.

Richard Hopkinson (8)
Eccleston Primary School

Happy

I am happy when I have a friend,
I am happy when I get an animal,
I am happy when I get presents for my birthday,
I am happy when I go horse riding and mucking out.

Danielle Hilton (9)
Eccleston Primary School

The Weirdest Animals In The World

Once I saw a fish
Alive in a dish!

I saw a lion
Using an iron!

I saw a croc
Eating a rock!

I saw a cat
Squashing a bat!

I saw a cow,
Take a bow!

I saw a pig,
Wearing a wig!

I saw a hen,
Counting to ten!

I saw a bird
Saying a word!

Alex Weetman (9)
Eccleston Primary School

I Am Brave

I am brave,
I am strong,
I am brave, when I hurt my tongue.
I am a muscle man,
I am like a rubber band,
I am Dan the man
Like a rubber man.
I am like Superman,
I am like a laser man.

Daniel Eccles (8)
Eccleston Primary School

My Monster

I have a monster 50-foot tall
I have a monster who almost ate Skinny Paul.

I have a monster whose favourite toys are cars,
But all I have are chocolate bars.

I have a monster who runs down the motorway,
If you mess with him you'll pay.

I have a monster that looks like a T-rex,
Who has a baby named Lex.

I have a monster blue and green,
He didn't like the dolls I've seen.

I have a monster who can fly,
But someone shot him and he didn't die.

I have a monster who plays with a house for a football.
I love my monster and he always loves me more.

Michael Bleasdale (8)
Eccleston Primary School

Animals

Pigs are smelly
Horses are clean
Cows are the ones with the big fat belly.

Cats jump up high
Dogs pounce around
Hamsters sleeping
Birds tweeting.

Everybody likes animals,
They're the best things in the world.
Without animals where would we be?

Chloe Miller (8)
Eccleston Primary School

Wake Up

Wake up!
Let your dreamy eyes
Open onto the day.

Wake up!
Let your soft head
Come up.

Wake up!
Let your little legs
Stretch to the sky and back.

Wake up!
Let you little mind
Open up into somewhere.

Wake up!
Let your hard tongue be moving
And let your day go.

Ellie Forrest (8)
Eccleston Primary School

Football

I like football
Because you can
Score all you want.

I like football
Because I am
Always in goal.

I fly to the sky
And then
Hit the ground.

Most of the time
I save
All the goals.

Calvin Merry (8)
Eccleston Primary School

Bored

When I'm bored I look up to the sky
And what do I see up there?
I see white clouds of fluff
Made out of cotton wool
And a navy blue thing up there.

When I'm bored I read a book
And what do I read in the book?
I read a story about three children
Who go on exciting adventures
But none are like mine.

When I'm bored in the car
I just sit and wait
And listen to my CDs
And then wonder
What will happen to me next.

Alex Bennett-Forshaw (9)
Eccleston Primary School

Brave

I'd feel brave
If I swam
With a shark.

I'd feel brave,
If I jumped
Out of an aeroplane.

I'd feel brave,
If I dived
Off Mount Everest.

I'd feel brave,
If I did something
Without any help.

Rebecca Bradley (8)
Eccleston Primary School

The Storm

Flashing lightning,
Twinkling, sparkling.
Lots of thunder,
Bashing, clashing.

Wind and rain,
Blowing, flooding.
People screaming,
Dashing, running.

The storm's ended,
The sun's coming out.
The clouds are parting,
There are people about.

Alice Davies (8)
Eccleston Primary School

Cars

Big cars,
Small cars,
Fords, Minis, Peugeots
And Citroëns
Are all good
To me.
Rally cars,
Racing cars,
Fast cars,
Slow cars,
Smashed cars.

Kyle Hesketh (9)
Eccleston Primary School

Mad About Cars

Super cars,
Leather interior.
High speed engine
Revs like mad.

Performance cars
Have good wheels.
Ah, watch out
There's steam in the air.

General cars,
Lots of miles,
Lots of gallons,
Sets off slow.

Haunted cars
None around
Everything silly
All the time.

Ryan Banks (9)
Eccleston Primary School

My Monster

My monster
Lives under my bed.
He's purple, green, blue and red.

My monster
Has a car.
He drove it back to his own star.

I miss my monster,
I wish he was here,
I need him
Tell me if he's near!

James Frankland (8)
Eccleston Primary School

Wish, Wish, Wish

I wish I could be a pop star,
I wish I could change my name.
I wish that I had a very long car,
I wish I'd never get the blame.

I wish I lived near a swimming pool,
I wish I could do everything right.
I wish I didn't have to go to school,
I wish I could stay up late at night.

I wish I could do magic tricks,
I wish I could always be a star.
I wish I could make a den from sticks,
I wish I could run really far.

I wish I could have whatever I wanted,
I wish I could have straight hair.
I wish I could grow whatever I planted,
I wish I could fly up in the air.

Lisa Quickfall (8)
Eccleston Primary School

No

No more playing in the sun,
No more eating a big fat bun.

No more having water fights,
No more playing in the nights.

No more fishing in the stream,
No more eating ice cream.

No more riding bikes in the street,
No more running in bare feet.

No! No! November!

Craig Everton (9)
Eccleston Primary School

Fireworks

A bright light
A pretty pattern
Whistling, whizzing,
Sizzling, swirling
Fireworks.

Matthew Thompson (8)
Eccleston Primary School

The Blue Whale

The big blue whale,
Slaps its long wide tail,
As it swims through the silent sea.

Weighing two tonnes when it's born,
Loving seas that are so warm,
It's the largest creature on Earth.

When meal time comes,
It eats one or two tonnes,
Of delicious, but tiny krill.

Avoiding the slaughter,
As it swims through the water,
By the great and fierce killer whale.

As it migrates to the north,
Its haunting song goes forth,
Its future, still uncertain.

Rachael Worrall (10)
Greenhill Primary School

What's Friendship?

Friendship is like the breeze,
You can't hold it,
Smell it,
Taste it,
Or know when it's coming and going,
But you will always love it
And you'll always know when it's there.
It may come and then go,
But you will always know it'll be back watching over you soon.

You will age and so will they,
But your friendship stays, strong and true forever.

Charlotte Snell (11)
Greenhill Primary School

A Meal

We could go to a restaurant
and have a spicy curry
or we could go to McDonald's
and have a McFlurry.

We're not going to the chippy
because I don't like mushy peas.
We could go to Pizza Hut
'Double cheese please.'

We might go to KFC
and have a chicken breast.
Oh dear!
We're not going any more
so I won't mention the rest.

Matthew Brock (11)
Greenhill Primary School

Summer Comes, Spring Goes

The sweet smell of spring,
Has gently run away,
But now the summer heat is here to stay.

Spring met her sister, Summer,
And said, 'While I fade and
You grow stronger, all the
Flowers will grow longer.'

Now the spring has gone to bed,
Her sister Summer said, 'I miss my
Sister I wish I'd said goodbye.'

Now Autumn has taken over,
All the flowers have lost their power,
Well now Summer is done,
I bet Autumn is having fun!

Lauren Farrow (9)
Greenhill Primary School

The Volcano

The volcano screamed and shook as it awoke,
The Earth groaned and trembled as it erupted.
It vomited out molten lava like an angry dragon,
Burning trees and melting rocks, roaring with rage,
Rumbling as it rolls rocks down its side.
It takes a trip to the sea, taking half the town with it.
Still vomiting out vile lava over its victims via the valleys.
It burns down bushes, blackening them,
Banishing them from the Earth.
It's getting tired again now, starting to yawn
As slowly it stops vomiting and roaring.
It closes its mouth and blinks before
It shuts its eyes and falls asleep till next time
When it will wake up to unleash itself
And commit another crime.

Joshua Rowlands (11)
Greenhill Primary School

List Poem

Anger is . . .
Anger is slamming a door shut,
Anger is lightning,
Anger is fire,
Anger is someone telling you off,
Anger is . . .

Happiness is . . .
Happiness is playing netball,
Happiness is making new friends
Happiness is the sun shining,
Happiness is going to a friend's sleepover,
Happiness is a new toy
Happiness is . . .

Nervousness is . . .
Nervousness is a test,
Nervousness is my dog running off,
Nervousness is a storm,
Nervousness is doing puzzles,
Nervousness is . . .

Amy Quigley (9)
Greenhill Primary School

My Love Poem

You are beautiful, you are my love,
You're as sweet as a little white dove.
You are smart, I'd love to give you a hug,
You're cute and cuddly unlike a bug.
You are wonderful, I'd love to braid your hair,
You are the best, you're just like a teddy bear.
You are the greatest, I am never blue,
Because I've got you!

Mark Dean (10)
Greenhill Primary School

Babies

Babies are beautiful,
They come in girls and boys,
Everything about them is beautiful,
Even their toys.

Babies cry and
We don't know why,
We try to help them,
We try and we try.

Babies are beautiful, I can't describe why,
When we say goodbye, they cry,
Their pretty little hands and cute little noses,
Their chubby little fingers and adorable little faces.

They start to smile and to crawl,
Best of all is when they stop to bawl,
First nursery, then pre-school,
Then up, up and away.

Sarah Kidd (9)
Greenhill Primary School

Sweet Nothing
(The tale of a child who was bullied)

My life was filled with happiness,
My life was filled with glee,
But all of a sudden you came along
And ruined my life and me.
You didn't mean to hurt,
You didn't mean to cause the pain,
But you did make my life dirt.
The pain was too intense
My mind could not survive,
So I'm glad to say to you,
'I've gone now. Goodbye!'

Rebecca Pollard (10)
Greenhill Primary School

Brownies

Brownies earn badges,
Brownies make new friends,
Brownies go to church parades
And that's not where it ends!

Brownies go on camping trips,
When they're nine years old,
Brownies meet on dark, dark nights
And Brownies get enrolled.

Brownies think about their God,
They always have good fun,
Arts and crafts, tig and things
Always can be done.

So why don't you be one?

Saffron Emily Burgess (7)
Greenhill Primary School

Happiness

Games make me happy,
My parents too,
Everything makes me happy,
So do you.

Action games are my favourite,
Adventure games too,
Car games are the best,
I just can't choose.

Everything makes me happy,
Everyone's the best,
I like everyone,
Especially you!

Robert Bromley (11)
Greenhill Primary School

A War In Medieval Times

Stab with a dagger,
Chop with a sword,
Shoot with an arrow,
Down the east ward.

Captured by the enemy,
Taken to prison.
Tortured and whipped,
And sent on a mission.

Then the land is taken . . .

Ryan Holmes (9)
Greenhill Primary School

Happiness

Happiness is a new PS2 game,
Happiness is winning a cricket match,
Happiness is playing with my friends,
Happiness is watching wrestling,
Happiness is my pet dog,
Happiness is a new pair of trainers.

Haydn Brown (10)
Greenhill Primary School

Happiness Is . . .

Happiness is a warm home,
Happiness is a cuddly toy,
Happiness is a friendship,
Happiness is passing an exam,
Happiness is . . .

Georgia Whittles (9)
Greenhill Primary School

What Is The Moon?

It is a big ball of cheese,
    Floating on top of a Hovis cracker.
It is a giant gobstopper,
    Being sucked in a tunnel.
It is the face of a snowman,
    On a dark black sky.
It is a cream wall,
    In a cold, empty room.
It is white powder puffed on a face
    In a ballroom.

Lauren Madden (10)
Greenhill Primary School

What Is Snow?

Snow is the icing on your birthday cake,
Snow is sheep's wool falling from the sky,
It is sugar being sprinkled on your cereal,
Snow is a nice cosy white blanket on your bed,
Snow is feathers falling from a pillow in the sky,
Snow is a great white T-shirt covering the Earth.

Kate Allanson (10)
Greenhill Primary School

Happiness Is . . .

Happiness is completing a game,
Happiness is to have a new car,
Happiness is going to a sleepover,
Happiness is staying up late,
Happiness is going to a concert.

Habib Shama (9)
Greenhill Primary School

Dolphins

Dolphins, dolphins, clever, clever,
Working all day doing tricks,
Swimming around touching the ground,
Hitting a ball with their nose,
There they go loop-the-loop,
There they go through the hoop,
Round and round they go,
Their tail goes to and fro,
Being friendly all day long,
This is the end of our song.

Amy Dunn (9) & Jennifer Naisbett (8)
Greenhill Primary School

Happiness Is . . .

Happiness is laughter,
Happiness is dolphins swimming in the sea,
Happiness is a rainbow shining,
Happiness is horse riding,
Happiness is summer,
Happiness is Sports Day,
Happiness is when it's snowing.

Rachael Lytham (9)
Greenhill Primary School

Horses

I like horses, I think they're cool,
Oh look he's so cute,
Clip-clop go his hooves,
When they go fast, they are bouncy,
Their faces are so sweet,
Sometimes they are very cheeky.

Esther Morrissey (8)
Greenhill Primary School

Mr Tiger

Mr Tiger why are you bearing your teeth like that?
Mr Tiger why are you staring at me like that?
Mr Tiger why have you put me in your mouth like that?
Mr Tiger why are we heading south like that?
Mr Tiger why are we in your den like that?
Mr Tiger why are there bones from men like that?
Mr Tiger why does your wife look like she needs her tea like that?
Mr Tiger why are you grinning at me like that?

Oh I see!

Caitlin Cole (8)
Greenhill Primary School

Summer's Sunny, Winter's Snowy

Winter's going, summer's coming,
The sea is coming out,
The coldness isn't there,
Time to get outdoors,
Don't have to wear your coats any longer,
The sun is coming out, the winter's going away,
Time to come out and play,
Get your paddling pool out and play.

Hannah Simons (8)
Greenhill Primary School

Pets

Billy is my rabbit,
Who is fluffy and grey,
Minty is my hamster,
Who tries to run away,
Minty is nocturnal,
Billy is not,
Have you got any pets at home?
Have you or not?

Hannah Worrall (7)
Greenhill Primary School

On A Jolly Day

Dazy-gazy flowers,
Smiling at the sun,
Enjoying all the weather,
And having so much fun.

Lots and lots of smells,
From all the beautiful flowers,
Sniffing, sniffing all the way,
And gazing at the towers.

The flowers in the hills,
Are such a beautiful sight,
When it is a windy day,
You might just see a kite.

Emily Fuller (8)
Greenhill Primary School

Lion Cub Dreams

I am just a lion cub
A male I am
I am really in the swing
Just as much as I will be
When I am king.

I am just a lion cub
A female I am
And when I am queen
I am not going to be mean
Because I'll have a mind
To tell me what's kind.

Elizabeth Alblas (7)
Greenhill Primary School

Happiness Is . . . Nervousness Is . . .

Happiness is . . .
Happiness is a foreign holiday,
Happiness is people smiling,
Happiness is friends to talk to,
Happiness is a family,
Happiness is . . .

Nervousness is . . .
Nervousness is a SATs test,
Nervousness is your first football match,
Nervousness is Sports Day,
Nervousness is . . .

Jenny Keen (9)
Greenhill Primary School

My Dog Pepper - The Scaredy Cat

My dog Pepper is as big as a house
But sometimes she's as scared as a mouse,
Whenever we get the brush out to sweep,
Pepper runs away to hide and she will only peep.

Pepper is scared of my remote control car,
And when it starts to move, she runs very far,
When fireworks explode at night,
Pepper shivers with fright.

Pepper hates lettuce for tea but
She really loves me.

Megan Giffard (7)
Greenhill Primary School

My Dog

My dog's name is Sandy,
She is the colour of sand,
My dog is funny and she acts like a bunny,
It is quite funny,
My dog is as thick as a log, she runs around
Like a demented frog,
My dog licks me because she loves me
And leaves my hand all wet,
And when she is poorly, she goes to the vet.

Matthew Brown (7)
Greenhill Primary School

Wear A Smile

I am a happy, happy face,
I am in a happy place,
Don't feel sad,
You will be glad,
Put on a smile and not a frown,
Then people will be glad that
You're around when they see a smile.

So put on a happy face!

Alexandra Rose White (7)
Greenhill Primary School

The Easter Bunny

There's the Easter bunny,
Who hardly touches the floor,
As he hops and bounces through the streets,
And enters every door.
But do you know what he gives you?
It's round and sweet and yummy,
It's a chocolate Easter egg
To put inside your tummy.

Anna Tollitt (7)
Greenhill Primary School

What Is Snow?

Snow is a white tissue
Dropped to the ground by a giant.

It is icing sugar
Sprinkled from Heaven.

It is a blanket
Laid over the ground.

It is a layer of clotted cream
On top of an apple.

Ruth Merrick (10)
Greenhill Primary School

Cheetahs

Cheetahs are very fast animals,
Horrible animals they can be,
Everyone can get injured,
Everyone can be killed,
Turn and you'll see,
Everyone run,
Run away!

Sarah Pollard (7)
Greenhill Primary School

Summer Is Fun

Summer is great,
Especially when the sun comes up,
Every single day,
I love it when the birds start singing,
I forget what I am doing,
It's just so great at
Summertime.

Charlotte Dunkley (8)
Greenhill Primary School

Nibbles

C ute little Nibbles
R unning around
E eating nuts
A nd digging the ground,
T eeth like razors
U nder his nose
R each in with cardboard, and
E verything goes.

Reece Spencer (9)
Greenhill Primary School

What Is . . . The Moon?

The moon is a giant golf ball
Floating in the sea.

It is lots of snowballs crammed into one,
It is very shiny and bright.

It is a rocky shell that spaceships land on.

Rebecca Carr (10)
Greenhill Primary School

Happiness

Happiness is work,
Happiness is a dog or a puppy,
Happiness is a lot of food,
Happiness is a lot of snow,
Happiness is playing on my PlayStation,
Happiness is my family.

Tomas Helliwell (9)
Greenhill Primary School

Colourful Moods

When people say 'I'm feeling *blue*,'
It really means they're sad.
But when they say, 'I'm in the *pink*,'
They're happy, lively and glad,
It's strange when people say things,
Like envy turns you *green*,
Or someone's turned ghostly *white*!
At frightening things they've seen,
The colours are strange that people go
Or say that they have been,
But I have the same colour skin,
Whatever mood I'm in!

Danni Critchley (11)
Greenhill Primary School

My Favourite Pirate

My favourite pirate has a long brown beard,
My favourite pirate is very fierce,
My favourite pirate has a patch over one eye,
My favourite pirate hates saying goodbye,
My favourite pirate had lots of treasure,
My favourite pirate is collecting tape measures.

Samantha Spencer (9)
Greenhill Primary School

Neil

There once was a banana called Neil,
Who got squished by a huge wheel,
His friends came along who were posh,
And said, 'You're in quite a squash!'

Jacob Eardley-Dutton (9)
Greenhill Primary School

I Like Easter

I like Easter,
It's the time that I was born,
I should have come four weeks later,
But I arrived on Good Friday morn,
Was it the thought of Easter bunnies
Or lunch with turkey legs?
It may be that I just love
Chocolate and
Came to get my eggs!

Sophie Stone Smith (8)
Greenhill Primary School

Fire

See the flames, hot as the sun
Orange, yellow and red,
Like a beach with
Its warm colours.
Beautiful to behold but
Dangerous to touch,
Its fiery flames will torture you,
With terrible pain.

Chloe Walker (10)
Greenhill Primary School

The Storm

Tearing the heart out of the town,
The thunder roars like an angry lion,
The lightning screams like a scared child,
The tree branches fastly running across the ground,
The rain lashes the ground fiercely,
The wind howls mournfully.

Carly Lockey (11)
Greenhill Primary School

What Is . . . A Crater?

It's a giant's football
> Stuck in the ground.
It's a giant's footstep
> As deep as an ocean.
It is an invisible piece of ground
> That everybody falls down.
It is a big rabbit's home
> That it dug out.
It is a shepherd's pit
> For keeping sheep.
It is a giant's pond
> That is looked at every day.

Amy Smith (9)
Greenhill Primary School

What Is Snow?

A sprinkle of salt
On the rooftops.

Icing sugar
Like a carpet.

Talcum powder
On the window ledges.

White beads falling from a string
In the murky sky.

Falling feathers
From a pillow in the sky.

Flour being sprinkled
Through a sieve.

Rachel Reay (9)
Greenhill Primary School

The Snowman

The snowman was scared
He would melt on a hot day
And someone would come and
Take it away
And the strong wind would come
And blow him away.
If it lands it would smash like a smashed egg
And could be a puddle on the ground
When he goes he says
'I will come back again next year.'

Mohmed Valibhai (8)
Hawthorns Junior School

Snowman

Make the snowman talk and walk,
Please do not make him melt,
Otherwise he will fall onto the ground,
When it rains he will melt,
When we go out to play in the snow,
It will be gone,
Then we will be sad.

Muhammad Chopdat (8)
Hawthorns Junior School

Stars

Look in the sky, you will see a star,
Stars shine brightly,
Stars are very tiny,
They look very pretty in the sky,
Everyone knows that the stars are bright.

Sonia Khalid (8)
Hawthorns Junior School

Fireworks

F ireworks can be dangerous
I t is important to keep children away from the fireworks
R emember to keep pets indoors,
E njoy watching fireworks
W ork together to not let any accidents happen
O nly light fireworks in a safe place
R emember to stay well back from the fireworks
K eep fireworks in a metal box with a lid
S parklers should be kept in a bucket of water
                                    when they have finished.

Stay safe!

Zenab Hussain (10)
Hawthorns Junior School

Snowman

Snowman, snowman, please don't go,
Snowman, snowman, I'll cry if you go,
Snowman, snowman if you go, I will miss you so much,
I wish you didn't go, please don't go,
I wish you didn't have to go, I will miss you.

Shabnam Rehman (8)
Hawthorns Junior School

Snowman

Snow is bright is shines at night,
Snow is light and shines at night,
In the dark it glows and it
Says tip-tap, tip-tap.
It melts with the rain showering down,
And when you try to touch it, it disappears.

Ikra Hassain (8)
Hawthorns Junior School

Fireworks

F ireworks are fun if you stick by the rules,
I njuries can happen if you play with fireworks,
R ockets are dangerous if you don't use them properly,
E very time you light fireworks put them in a metal box,
W atch out for any stray fireworks,
O nly adults should light fireworks,
R emember to keep fireworks in a metal box,
K eep well away from fireworks that are lit,
S parklers should be put in a bucket of water when finished.

Sheikl Iqbal (11)
Hawthorns Junior School

Fireworks

F ireworks are dangerous,
I njuries can happen,
R emember the rules,
E very firework is dangerous,
W e must not go very close,
O nly adults light fireworks,
R ules are important,
K eep pets indoors,
S tay safe.

Adil Hussain (10)
Hawthorns Junior School

Untitled

On a dark night,
The sky has some light,
For there are some shimmering stars,
I can see,
I wink at them and they wink at me,
They are happy dancing in the sky,
Glittering and sparkling in my eye.

Humaira Khan (8)
Hawthorns Junior School

Houses

My house is hot, my attic is cold,
My hands are shivering so are yours,
My eyes are sore, everybody knows,
I am still changing my clothes,
It is chilly right up here,
Do you know what we could hear?
A roaring tiger that is clear,
It is spooky right up here,
Do you think I will cry?
Oh yes! My eyes!

Muneeba Khalil (7)
Hawthorns Junior School

My Snowman

My snowman is as fat as a cat,
And as soft as a rabbit,
He is worried because in summer he will melt,
He is feeling sorry for himself,
He feels like a lonely teddy bear,
When nobody says goodbye,
He does not want to melt,
He does not want to leave,
His old friends behind!

Obeid Soge (8)
Hawthorns Junior School

Razee - An Acrostic Poem

R aring to go and full of energy
A lways football mad
Z ooming like a rocket!
E ntering places no one wants to go
E ntertaining.

Razee Khaliq (10)
Hawthorns Junior School

Fireworks

F ireworks can be fun but dangerous,
I f you touch the top of a sparkler you may burn your hand,
R emember keep bonfires away from houses, fences, etc,
E very Bonfire Night remember to keep pets indoors,
W e must not sell fireworks to children under 18 years old,
O nly adults should light fireworks,
R emember to light a firework in a safe place,
K eep fireworks in a metal box with a lid
S afety means to stick with the rule.

Zulkernain Hussain (10)
Hawthorns Junior School

Fireworks

F lames can be dangerous,
I njuries can happen,
R emember, remember the 5th of November,
E veryone can have fun,
W atch fireworks and play safe,
O nly adults should light fireworks,
R emember the rules,
K eep away from fireworks,
S afety means stick with the rules.

Abdul Gaffar Aslam (11)
Hawthorns Junior School

Space

Space is as dark as a large thundercloud,
It is as quiet as a library
With aliens as tall as trees,
Spaceships travel as fast as a cheetah chasing a tiger,
It is as silent as a feather floating to the ground.

Akmal Ali (9)
Hawthorns Junior School

Fireworks

F ireworks can be dangerous,
I njuries have happened in the past,
R emember to keep pets indoors,
E mergencies can happen,
W atch fireworks from a far distance,
O nly adults should light fireworks,
R ules should be kept,
K eep bonfires away from houses, fences, etc,
S tay safe!

Zubare Sidik (10)
Hawthorns Junior School

Foreign Lands

When I climbed over the garden wall,
I saw a dragon so angry,
Through a looking glass,
I am a knight,
Coming to slay the dragon,
With my shiny silver sword,
And so I did and I never ever
Saw a dragon again.

Tayyib Hussain (8)
Hawthorns Junior School

Foreign Lands

When I looked over the garden wall,
I saw a castle,
A princess called me,
With a lantern in her hand,
She was tramping towards me,
On her white horse,
The ostler came with her of course.

Taniya Hussain (9)
Hawthorns Junior School

Clock O Clay

In the cowslip pips I lie,
I hidden from the buzzing fly,
While green grass beneath me lies,
Pearled with dew like fishes' eyes,
Here I lie a clock o clay,
Waiting for the time o clay.

While the forest quakes surprise,
And the wild wind sobs and sighs,
My home rocks as like to fall,
On its pillar green and tall,
When the pattering rain drives by,
Clock o clay keeps warm and dry.

Day by day and night by night
All the week I hide from sight
In the cowslips pips I lie,
In the rain warm and dry
Day and night, night and day
Red, black spotted clock o clay

My home shakes in wind and showers,
Pale green pillar topped with flowers,
Bending at the wild wind's breath,
Till I touch the grass beneath
Here I live, lone clock o clay,
Watching for the time of day.

Faheema Mehboob Adam (10)
Hawthorns Junior School

Friendship

Sharing and caring,
Is what friendship is all about.

No matter how big or how small,
A friend's act of kindness,
Always leaves a lashing touch of
Gold in the heart.

No matter how different friends are,
Or how far apart,
The sunshine and happiness,
Which they lend,
Always mend the gaps between them.
Friends are forever!

Mariya Shaikh (11)
Hawthorns Junior School

Foreign Land

When I peep over the garden wall
I see a magical land,
Where there's a duck pool as
Shiny as a looking glass,
And tall, lush straight green soggy grass,
The steeds in their stalls,
Gently neigh as he calls.

An ostler tramping up the dusty street,
I wonder whom he will meet,
A winding highway,
How many footsteps have trodden on you today?

Junaid Asghar (9)
Hawthorns Junior School

Fireworks

F ireworks can be dangerous,
I t is important that children keep away from fireworks,
R emember not to light fireworks near children,
E mergencies can happen,
W e should make sure our pets are kept indoors,
O nly over 18's should buy the fireworks and sparklers,
R ockets and other fireworks are very dangerous because
    they can cause serious injuries and keep children well away
                       and children under 3 years old,
K eep your pets, children, babies well away from fireworks,
S erious incidents can happen sometimes especially
                       on firework night.

Shamim Chopdat (11)
Hawthorns Junior School

Fireworks

F ireworks are dangerous, don't play with them,
I f fireworks shoot out at you, you run or hide,
R ed is the colour of dangerous fireworks,
E xtra special colours
W ater fireworks and play safe,
O n Bonfire Night, stand back from the fire,
R ockets are dangerous but good to see,
K eep fireworks in a metal tin with a lid,
S tay away from bonfires play a game that
                Doesn't involve *fireworks*
                Play safe and stick to the rules!

Aqib Butt (11)
Hawthorns Junior School

Fireworks

F ireworks are cool but dangerous,
I njuries can happen if you are not careful,
R ules are important so don't break them,
E verybody should play safe,
W atch fireworks from a safe distance,
O nly let adults light fireworks,
R emember fireworks can cause body damage,
K eep fireworks in a metal container with a lid,
S parklers should go in a bucket of water.

Ebrahim Chand (11)
Hawthorns Junior School

Fireworks

F ireworks are dangerous,
I f you're younger than 18, keep away,
R emember to keep fireworks in a metal box with a lid,
E very time you light a firework do it with a fuse,
W icked bad accidents can happen if you go back to a lit firework,
O nly light one firework at a time,
R emember to put sparklers in a bucket of water when finished,
K eep pets indoors,
S tay in a safe place.

Sundus Siddiqui (11)
Hawthorns Junior School

Snow

Snowman melting,
In the morning sun,
We had good times,
We had very good days,
I will miss you,
I wish you a merry Christmas.

Kushof Hussain (7)
Hawthorns Junior School

Foreign Lands

I see a puddle and imagine the sea,
I see multicoloured shells and mermaids
Combing their hair,
I see the magic sand moving into the sea
And pirates chanting in their wooden ships,
Galloping steeds hastening across the sea,
Smugglers riding into their dark cave,
To count their golden money,
And look at their sparkling treasure.

Kulsum Hussain (9)
Hawthorns Junior School

Vegetables

Why should I eat vegetables when I don't like them?
I'm not a rabbit, but Mum thinks I am,
'They're full of vitamins,' my mum says,
But it doesn't make me like them,
Because I never ate vegetables
My skin peeled off and you could see my bones!
So be warned, my family and friends
If you don't eat your vegetables
This could happen to you!

Oliver Tomlinson (8)
Holden Clough Primary School

Friends

Friends, friends lots of friends,
Friends never break friends,
Friends invite you to their house,
Friends never fight each other,
Friends laugh and play jokes.

Imran Sheikh (8)
Holden Clough Primary School

Animals

Animals are great,
Every animal ate,
Some animals don't look so good,
But if they had their own hands they would,
Some animals are fast,
But some animals don't last,
Some animals are greedy,
No animals look weedy,
All animals have names,
But animals can't play games,
Do you have an animal?

Megan White
Holden Clough Primary School

The Winter Wind

The winter wind is cold and snowy,
The summer wind is rainy everywhere,
The spring wind is sweet and nice,
The autumn wind is rustling red leaves off.

The spring leaves are soft staying on the trees,
The winter leaves are off the trees having fees,
The summer leaves are ready to fall off,
The autumn leaves are all orangy-yellow.

Daniel Lanham (8)
Holden Clough Primary School

The Winter Wind

The winter wind is soft and sweet,
The clouds are as white as snow,
The trees are green with lots of leaves
And there are lots of things to know.

Ravina Jobanputra (8)
Holden Clough Primary School

Sea Makes Me Happy

Sea makes me happy,
Sea makes me happy,
Sea makes me happy,
Does it make you happy too?

Sea is rough,
Sea is tough,
Sea is calm,
Sea can be alarmed.

Sea makes me happy,
Sea makes me happy,
Sea makes me happy,
Does it make you happy too?

Sea is battering,
Sea is clattering,
Sea makes me happy,
Sea makes me happy,
Does it make you happy too?

Samuel Fleetwood Myles (7)
Holden Clough Primary School

The Winds

The summer wind
Is soft and sweet
But the winter wind
Is hard and rough.

The spring wind
Is a breeze
But the autumn
Wind is mischievous
And sweeps the leaves along.

Benjamin Peter Coleman (8)
Holden Clough Primary School

When Does Santa Come?

When does Santa come?
He comes in the night!
He comes in the night!
He softly and silently comes.

While little brown heads,
And Santa in his red,
Are so excited before they go to bed!

He cuts through the snow,
Like a ship through the foam,
While little, white snowflakes swirl.

Who tells him? No one knows,
But he comes down the chimney
Going 'Ho! Ho! Ho!'

He finds the bed side of each good boy and girl,
While Ruddolf waits
In the snowflakes which swirl.

He comes in the night!
He comes in the night!
He softly and silently comes!

While little brown heads
And Santa in his red,
Are so excited before they go to bed!

Ayesha Ul-haq (9)
Holden Clough Primary School

In The Sea

In the sea it is rather blue,
It has got fish in it too,
When you look in the big, blue sea,
It makes me happy as can be,
I like the big, blue sea,
Everyone does, don't we?

Matthew Taylor (8)
Holden Clough Primary School

My Pink Fluff Ball

My pink fluff ball is very good
Even though it's full of mud
It sometimes barks
And leaves marks
All over the house.

My pink fluff ball
Likes to wag her tail
She runs around when she hears the mail
If I light a candle she would sit normally
But when she wants to she runs up a tree.

You wouldn't think she's normal
But she's as normal as can be
Because she's
As freaky as a freckle face
As scary as the human race
As strange as a pea
As wacky as this poem!

Anna Elizabeth Davies (9)
Holden Clough Primary School

Dolphin

Dolphins live in the sea,
As choppy as can be,
They jump up and down,
Around and around,
In the big, wide, choppy sea.

Some people think they could bite,
And some wonder whether they sleep in the night,
Dolphins are smooth,
And they like to move,
In the big, wide, choppy sea.

Hannah Margaret Millin (8)
Holden Clough Primary School

Skeleton!

A skeleton is not just one bone,
They go Direct Line to get a loan,
They can either go to Hell or Heaven,
They might even die at ninety-seven.

There's ribs, thigh and spine,
One used to be mine,
Skeletons are now all dead,
Underground coffins are their beds.

Skeletons are piles of bones,
Some are exactly like skeleton clones,
They are dead, dead, dead,
They are in their bed.

Sarah Mellor (8)
Holden Clough Primary School

My Dog Barthez

My dog Barty,
Likes to party,
And when he's got a bone,
He likes to be alone.

He likes a walk,
And a little talk,
He wears a coat,
But doesn't like boats.

When he's in a mood,
It means he wants some food,
And he's grey and white,
And starts lots of fights.

Emma Walton (9)
Holden Clough Primary School

Whales In The Sea

W hales are as big as a mountain,
H eavy, very heavy,
A very heavy creature they are,
L ong, big, high and wide,
E verybody has to go see him,
S mall when they are born.

I n the sea they eat krill,
N early get ill.

T hey go under the water for 30 minutes,
H e doesn't pay the bill when he gets the krill,
E lectric eels get scared.

S mall when the krill get eaten,
E at krill and shrimp,
A lways looking forward to a drink.

Dina Mardania (8)
Holden Clough Primary School

Blue Whales

Blue whales such lovely creatures,
Blue whales are always in water,
Blue whales eat krill and shrimps,
Blue whales loudest animal on Earth,
Blue whale as big as a tree,
You can never fit into a dish,
They have big, sharp teeth,
They do not bite, they do not bite,
But they are enormous,
Not tiny, not tiny,
You should like lovely blue whales,
Whales swimming in the blue sea.

Rachel Halliday (7)
Holden Clough Primary School

Blue Whales

Blue whales swim everywhere,
Joy and happiness
Everywhere,
Beautiful noises,
Calm seas,
Blue whales swim everywhere.

It's the blue whale
Swimming with pride
Swimming with females
To catch the tide.

Blue whales swim everywhere,
Jumping up and down
They eat krill, fish and seals,
Oh, all so bliss.

Georgia Main (9)
Holden Clough Primary School

Whales

Blue whales are big,
Grey whales are grey,
Killer whales are killers,
I hope you're not too.

The sperm whale has a huge brain,
It's probably more clever than you,
It swims in the sea,
And picks up all the stones.

At night they come up and dive,
They're calm and gentle.

They want to join the human race,
So let them be your friend, and let them be.

Clarice Jean Lee-Alker (9)
Holden Clough Primary School

Whales, Whales

Whales, whales,
Can you see them in the sea,
Prancing, dancing under the sea,
For everyone to see.
Whales, whales
They are fascinating in many ways
And are under estimated.
They are not predictors or nasty,
They are beautiful in every way,
Whales, whales,
Are all around you to keep you safe
And they will never harm you,
So look out for the most beautiful
Thing on Earth,
So the poem said.

George Dalton (9)
Holden Clough Primary School

Whales

Blue whales are 80-100 feet,
The blue whales like the heat,
Nar whales hold their breath for about 7-20 minutes,
The Nar whale has a limit.

Mike whales have a white band on their flipper,
I give them some knickers,
Whales sometimes dive,
But they always glide.

Some are blue,
People say they smell of pooh.

Naomi Fletcher (8)
Holden Clough Primary School

Whales, Whales

Whales, whales you see me,
I am in the large blue sea.
Krill krill such stinky krill,
I cannot stay still, still, still.
Whales have enormous teeth,
And eats slices of beef,
They are the biggest animals on Earth,
And are colourful at birth,
They do flips,
But do not do splits,
They are shiny and big,
And they do not dig,
Whales, whales, you see me,
I am in the large, blue sea.

Chloe Louise Wyatt (9)
Holden Clough Primary School

Whales

In the deep blue sea,
If you can see,
You might be able to see a whale,
With a gigantic piece of blubber,
In the deep blue sea,
If you can see,
There are Mike whales with
A pointed snout,
Beluga whales have a pair of tiny eyes,
They have a melon on their head,
Whales are the biggest animals on Earth,
But are small at birth,
If you give a whale a gift,
They will dance for you.

Nikita Patel (8)
Holden Clough Primary School

Whales In The Sea

Whales in the sea
Come to me
And look at me
Whales in the sea.

Some whales are big
And some whales are small
But they do not shop in the mall.

Some whales feed on krill
Some whales don't kill
Some whales will.

The blue whale is blue
Whales do not use glue
Some whales have a friend.

Whales in the sea
Come to me
And look at me
Whales in the sea.

Samuel Wellfair (7)
Holden Clough Primary School

Whales

Blue whales are big,
Hump backs have humps,
Killer whales eat fish,
Nar whales have a carrot nose.

Grey whales are nice,
Dolphins are cute,
Right whales have white patches,
And they swim in the sea.

Aidan Quinn (8)
Holden Clough Primary School

Class

'Shut up!
Shut up!

Yes that includes you Natasha.
Stop Natasha!
Dickey, turn your watch off.
Alex 11,505 points off for throwing a stink bomb at me.
Jack wash your hands after you've been to the loo.
Dickey, stop hitting people's bums.
Peter stop talking about garlic bread.
Mark stop eating!
Becky stop messing with your hair.
Charlotte stop talking about 'Footballers' Wives'.
Matty stop talking rude.
Jake, stop talking rude!'

Matthew Halliday (10)
Holden Clough Primary School

Whales

Whales are mammals, the biggest mammals,
Heavy whales are gigantic like three dinosaurs,
At the coldest sea on Earth blue whales live,
Like blue gales in the sea to eat krill,
Eating krill is one of their favourite things,
See to the whales you'll be interested, very,
An enormous tail,
Too big to be true, it's time to squirt,
Said to squirt like a waterfall,
Be nice to whales while they are on ice,
Nice, nice, whales indeed, very indeed.

Alexander James Spencer (9)
Holden Clough Primary School

Milk Time

'Right children, come on!'
They still carry on
'Milk time now!'
It's like a mouse,
You could hear a pin drop in the dolls' house.

The milk's given out by Sue
Whilst that happens, Olli eats his shoe
Chris spills his milk and starts to cry
Dervish's mum comes and he says, 'Bye!'

Fred adds to his milk a banana
Some apples, oranges and a sultana
Then he put it in the Hoover
Turned it on and made it smoother.

Milk time is nearly over
When Jill jumps on my poor dog Rover
Rover retaliates and bites her bum
Now isn't milk time really fun?

Joshua Nolan (11)
Holden Clough Primary School

Whales

Whales are big but not short,
They can't go to the loo like you,
A whale is something that can't fit in a tank,
Some whales make some noise, loud, not quiet,
It is a mammal but something you can't fit in the zoo,
You can fit a kangaroo in the zoo,
Whales are unique,
Some have spots,
Some have long tongues,
But they all can swim.

Hamaad Yousaf (8)
Holden Clough Primary School

School Dinners

Oh no, it's that time of day,
I can't believe my mum had to pay.
I'm disgusted
The curry's busted.

The pizza's, grotty
The custard's snotty.

The soggy mushy peas
The coleslaw's infested with fleas.

The mashed potato, thick and lumpy,
The thought of it makes me grumpy.

Now I've realised I'm not the winner,
That's it! I'll make my own dinner.

Charlotte Louise Young (11)
Holden Clough Primary School

The Bees

Bees are clever,
Bees are yellow,
Bees are busy,
Bees are back,
Bees like honey.

Bees are bossy,
Bees are squashy,
Bees do sting,
Bees are squishy,
Bees, bees, don't hurt bees!

Jessica Dyson (8)
Holden Clough Primary School

Strawberry Dream

Strawberry dream is creamy,
Strawberry dream is a chocolate,
Strawberry dream is so sticky,
It is from the roses.

Strawberry dream my favourite,
Strawberry dream I eat all day,
Strawberry dream is pink not red,
I just eat and eat and eat,
Strawberry dream - yum-yum.

Archana Chauhan (8)
Holden Clough Primary School

The Writer Of This Poem

(Based on 'The Writer of This Poem' by Roger McGough)

The writer of this poem is
As tall as a tower,
As big as a horse,
As quiet as a mouse,
As busy as a bee.

As clever as a queen,
As silly as a clown,
As lovely as chocolate.

Emily Bleackley (8)
Holden Clough Primary School

Sports

S ally is great at football, far better than all the boys
P eter is great at running, he always wins all the races.
O liver is great at lacrosse, far better than the teacher
R achel is great at rounders, she always wins.
T homas is great at cricket, he always gets the most runs.
S ophie just thinks she's great at everything!

Kathryn Booth (11)
Holden Clough Primary School

Whales

Whales are bigger than a dinosaur,
They won't even fit through a door,
Whales don't come up for a long time,
Following them is their horrible slime,
Whales are the biggest animals on Earth,
But they are only small at birth,
They have enormous teeth,
Whales are also good for meat,
They eat lots of krill,
But they don't kill.

Yasmin Etches (9)
Holden Clough Primary School

Shining Stars

The moon shining,
Coloured planets in the sky,
Mars and Jupiter, Pluto, Mercury sparkling
Stars are glowing in the dark,
Like a mermaid dancing in the air,
How I wonder, do they do it?
But they are very beautiful,
They are like sugar floating in the air.

Stephen Crane (9)
Holden Clough Primary School

Whales

Some are blue
Some are grey
Some just fly away,
Up into the night sky
Where they have a little playground
And then go back down underground.

Luke Hirst (8)
Holden Clough Primary School

Times Tables

'Right, now class,
It's time for tables,
Quiet down!
It's time for tables

Michael Bouviey,
Your pen is not a plane,
Michael Bouviey!
Your pen isn't a plane!

Right, ten multiplied by ten,
Come class,
Ten lots of ten!
Class!

Do I have to tell you how to behave?
Shut up class!
Do I have to tell you how to behave?
Shut up!

Apu,
Do not drink while I'm speaking,
Apu!
Don't ignore me!

What is ten times ten?
Joseph,
Joseph!
What is ten times ten!

Sally,
This is not a hair salon,
Sally!
Stop it, instantly!

Richard,
Is it crucial to breathe so heavily?
Richard!
Stop breathing!

Nine times nine class?
Right, that's it!
No play times
For a week!

Richard Selby (11)
Holden Clough Primary School

We're Leaving

We're leaving this year
My eyes caught a tear
The new school's barely near
I'll miss Holden Clough.

I'll never forget the teachers
And the way they used to teach us
Sir, you're my favourite teacher
I'll miss Holden Clough.

Our playground's so wild
The weather's so mild
The teacher just smiled
I'll miss Holden Clough.

I'll miss my tray
But we're leaving today
Let's celebrate, hip hip hooray
I'll miss Holden Clough.

If I lose my homework, I can't pretend
Did that door have to end?
I hope I make friends
I'll miss Holden Clough.

This is the start
I don't feel smart.
Now I hate art
I do miss Holden Clough.

Charlotte Vaughan (10)
Holden Clough Primary School

Dinn-Dinns

'Erm Miss Crossbones dinn-dinns
'Yes Miss Crossbones dinn-dinns,'

'Come on don't push'
'Yeah, don't push.'

'Pushin' through the door'
'Yeah, pushin' through the door,'

'Hey, do you know the new dinner lady?'
'Yeah, I know the new dinner lady.'

'She says everything twice'
'Yeah, she says everything twice,'

'Hey our dinner's here'
'Yeah, our dinner's here.'

'Oh you two, stop saying everything twice.'
'Oh Sir, we're not saying owt twice.'

'Detention both of you!'
'Yes, detention!'

Divya Khilosia (11)
Holden Clough Primary School

Whales

The sperm whale sprays 50 feet,
I hope it has something nice to eat,
I know it's not as fast as cheetahs,
But it can dive up to 20-25 metres,
A whale at its birth,
Is the loudest creature on Earth,
The killer has white skin,
I hope it will win,
I wish myself luck,
Cos I want to be in the book.

Ben Bowker (8)
Holden Clough Primary School

Getting Late

Oh hurry up,
You're getting really late.
Get your school bag
And get your slate.

Oh hurry up,
You're getting really late.
Don't forget your lunch
Or your fruit punch.

Oh hurry up
You're getting really late.
Look, there's your mate!
Do your hair, it's in a right state.

Oh hurry up,
You're getting really late.
You'll get into trouble
By the teacher you hate.

Oh hurry up,
You're getting really late.
Quick, quick, you'd better run -
See you Kate!

Sejal Dhorajiwala (11)
Holden Clough Primary School

Whales

Whales are mammals, big mammals,
Whales are blue, light blue,
Whales weigh 54,000 kg
Whales are kind creatures,
Whales grow 54 feet long,
Whales are 6 foot long,
Whales eat squid,
Whales have 5 pairs of teeth.

Joseph Slifkin (8)
Holden Clough Primary School

Playtime

It's playtime, children running around in the playground,
Some screaming, doing their meanings.
One bumped its head, now they're dead!
Flying up to Heaven,
Oops! They fell.
Now they're in Hell, boiling hot.
In the demon's pot,
Here comes the Devil,
He's very evil.
Pours in the fire,
Calls me a baby crier.
Now I'm dead, the second time
And then I hear a loud chime.
Hell has had enough of me
They sent me up to Heaven with glee.

Amman Khan (11)
Holden Clough Primary School

School Dinners

Here it comes *slop* it's the twelve bean casserole,
I heard Neddy ate it all!
I hear Liam is about to die,
Just from eating a blueberry pie!

Harold got indigestion,
Just by eating the dinner lady's suggestion.
Oh great mushy peas,
I'd rather eat my dog's fleas.

Oh no, it's the ham
I actually like to eat some Spam.
Oh #@!? it's shepherd's pie.
Oh gosh! Why oh why, oh why?
That's it, I'm joining sandwiches,
Because of these dinner lady witches!

Joshua Ramiah (10)
Holden Clough Primary School

Playtime

Playtime draws near
So bring out the beer,
Alcohol free for me
Miss, I need a wee.

I'm glad I've got out
To escape from that clout,
I can't stand her talks
But I do like my walks.

Down in the hall
I met someone tall.
When we play cricket, he fields in the gully
But there was a downside,
He's the school bully.

Thank the Lord, he didn't hit me
Instead he just bit me.
It was just seconds till the bell went
I'll have to go before I get bent.
I'll have to think
Who I can beat at forty winks.

Matthew David Lewis (11)
Holden Clough Primary School

Science

'Oh no Mark, put on your safety glasses!
For that experiment you only need two masses,
Put in some baking powder,
And Matthew Halliday, can you shout a bit louder!
Look at all that smoke over there,
And you don't even look like you give a care!
That's it!
All down to the headteacher's office!'

Rebekah Choudhury (10)
Holden Clough Primary School

School Time

No! No! It's already school time,
I'm going to be late.
No, there goes my lemon and lime
Oh no, what's the date?

Only six streets away,
Hurry up! Hurry up!
I think it's Monday
Oh better zip my bag up.

Oh no, there's lots of dogs
Better run fast
Oh no, lot's of logs,
Yes, the dogs have gone past.

Oh wait it's only Saturday!

Jake Forrest (10)
Holden Clough Primary School

English

On Monday I had to read my poem out
But I surrendered and backed out

On Tuesday we had a test on Shakespeare
And my head, filled with fear

We've got to write an essay today
Luckily the teacher's out and away

With all these thoughts in my head
It makes me want to get to bed

English is just so cruddy
I'd rather play out and get muddy.

Mohammed Zubair Khan (11)
Holden Clough Primary School

The School Of Paranormality

There's a Yeti in Class Six,
Doing a DJ's mix.
And a monster in Class Two
With only one shoe.

There's a vampire in 4B
Playing with his one knee.
And an alien in the dining hall
Shrinking everyone ant-like, small.

There's a dragon in the play-pit,
Turning sand into grit.
And a werewolf in the computer room
Putting killer flowers into bloom.

There's a mummy in 11C
The same class as me.
And a wolfman teacher called Mr Phelp,
Who makes me shout *Help! Help! Help!*

Jack Mather (11)
Holden Clough Primary School

My Brother

I am a big fan of Tracy Beaker
Not like my brother who wants to be a streaker,
She can be nasty and horrible but in a polite way,
I would do anything to be her for a day.

There is a lot more to Tracy Beaker
Unlike my brother, who is a lot weaker,
With her short black curly hair
I think they make a lovely pair.

My brother is not being fair
But hey, I don't care.
Tracy Beaker is here to stay
So he can go away!

Taybah Gufar (8)
Holden Clough Primary School

Whales

Whales are massive creatures,
They go shopping and get tonnes of krill.
The funny thing is they don't pay a bill,
If they don't pay a bill they will get really ill.
Whales spin and win but they have a broken fin.
Whilst the humpback's song lasts for 30 minutes but it never wins.
If the toothed whale has something nice to eat,
It will spray 50 feet.
They have a lovely tea,
But I hope they don't eat me!

Neha Ahmed (8)
Holden Clough Primary School

Dreams

Am I evil or a heroine?
If I go to sleep then I will soon see,
Witches and dragons,
Goblins and toads
But it's fairies that I dream about most!

Fluttering and flying in the trees,
Skimming the waters of the seas.
Up and down
Side to side,
Where to go, I've got to decide!

Up in the sky
Or down below,
Where I am heading, I do not know.
Not another soul in sight,
It's drawing nearer to the end of the night.

Suddenly it's morning and I awake,
That dream has brought a smile to my face!

Amanda Wood (11)
Holy Infant & St Anthony School

Grandma

My grandma is nice
Like sugar and spice
Grandma gives me treats
When I'm good
She goes to church
She prays every day
She loves God
As she loves me
If I had no mum or dad
I wouldn't have a grandma
I love my grandma, the way she is
Instead of calling me Lauren
She calls me Angel Girl
When it's her birthday, we say
'Hip hip hooray,'
For the world's best grandma.

Lauren McKee (10)
Holy Infant & St Anthony School

Flowers

Flowers are pink,
Flowers are red.
All are pretty alive,
All are horrid when dead.

Flowers smell nice,
Flowers smell sweet.
Flowers are nice to look at
And they feel nice, like a velvet seat.

They grow sometimes fast,
They help some insects feed.
Without those little things in the world,
Some nice insects might not breed.

Matthew Jeffs (10)
Holy Infant & St Anthony School

My Family

This is my story,
I hope you listen well!
All sit down and concentrate
Because it's very hard to tell.

My dad makes me laugh
When I'm sad and bored,
He acts like a clown sometimes
And in his sleep, he snores!

My mum cooks the tea
And does the washing up.
She irons all the clothes
And does the rabbits' hutch.

My brother wants to be a chef
He cooks a lot at school,
He likes to go to football
And is very good at pool.

Then there's me
The princess of them all,
I am ten years old
And four feet tall.

Well now you've heard my story
And this is where it ends.
If you like my family -
Why not be my friend?

Hayley Walton (10)
Holy Infant & St Anthony School

My Family

My family is unusual
My family is so strange,
My mum is out all day long
And she always gets her pay.
My dad gets all the house chores
Cleaning, cooking and shopping too.

And then there's me.
I'm whacky and I'm crazy
I'm the weirdest in the world.
I'm up when the cockerel crows
And down when the sun is low.
Low as it can go.

All my aunts and all my uncles
Are exactly the same.
They are all into classical
None of it's rock.
My grandad is so special
Because he provided the love this family needs
My grandma is the funniest
As she knows all the jokes!

I like the way my family are
And I don't want them to change.
So now you've heard about my family -
What about yours?

Jane O'Rourke (10)
Holy Infant & St Anthony School

My Cat Charlie

My cat Charlie is special,
She sits in front of the TV.
She has her special chair
She sleeps all night and day.

She's grey and black,
The same as her twin.
Her face is nice and friendly
You can always tell them apart.

She never eats with the others,
She prefers to be alone.
She loves the heat of the sun
For she always sits in it.

Her favourite place is in her chair,
Nobody is allowed to sit in it!
She is my special cat and
I love her to bits.
For she is my special cat!

Stacey Gray (11)
Holy Infant & St Anthony School

Pebbles

Pebbles are funny, shaped and colourful,
They are smooth and soft and big and small.
And they sit on the beach covered with sand.
Then the tides wash them away
And are collected by the people.

Have you ever felt a pebble?
Go down to the seaside and see
What you can find.

Holly Howarth (9)
Holy Infant & St Anthony School

My Poem About Beth Gelert

The story that I am about to tell
Is about a hound dog, very brave.
He gave up his own poor, poor sad long life.
Today we can see him in a small grave.

In a town in Wales on a cold night,
'Watch my babe!' Llewellyn told his dog.
'I will be back soon, make sure he is safe.'
He went, disappearing in the fog.

When all was silent as a small, small mouse,
Some beast walked in through the creaky door.
A huge wolf! Gelert had seen! And they fought.
Finally, Wolf was dead on the floor.

Llewellyn walked in and saw all the blood,
Llewellyn thought Gelert had killed his babe,
He stuck a sharp sword into his heart.
But then he heard the cry of his young babe.

What have I done?' Llewellyn shouted out,
He was a hound dog so very brave.
Now we can see him near Colwyn Bay,
Peacefully sleeping in a small grave.

Megan Andrews (9)
Holy Infant & St Anthony School

The Stars

The stars are like jewels,
They sit in the night sky.
They help me find my way,
They will never die.
They will be there forever,
They will never-ever go.
I've told my part -
Tell me what you know?

Naomi Sarsfield (10)
Holy Infant & St Anthony School

The Teacher's Mistake

There's a school in Astley Bridge,
That's known for fun and games
And all the children that go there
Never get called silly names!

The very best class was Year 5,
Whose teacher was Mrs Oaks.
She taught the class all sorts of subjects
Told stories and lots of good jokes.

One day as she started the lesson,
She noticed the class was bare.
Not one single child was present
Not one single child was there!

So the teacher got up from her desk
And wandered about in the school,
But then she realised something
That made her such a fool!

On the desk in the headmaster's office,
An up-to-date calendar lay,
Which explained the reason behind things
Today was in fact, Saturday!

Amber Mayo (9)
Holy Infant & St Anthony School

Snow Drops

Snow, snow, fun to throw
Everywhere there's snow, snow, snow
You make a snowman
Or a ball you can throw.

Snow is fun for everyone
Snow, snow, beautiful snow
Falls at night and here in light
So out we run and go.

Molly Johnson (10)
Holy Infant & St Anthony School

The Start Of My Day

It's time for school get out your bed,
It's time to wake up your sleepy head.
Throw back the covers put my feet on the floor,
I'm heading for the bathroom door.

Wash my face brush my teeth,
Now dress myself it's time to eat.
I look at the clock, it's time to go
So my mum drives me to school nice and slow.

I get to school and wave goodbye,
And hope that the day will fly.
I meet my friends at the gate,
I didn't stop, it might be late.

The bell rings, we all line up
To the classroom in single file.
The teacher calls us, one by one
To tick our names now the day's begun.

Nicole Jones (10)
Holy Infant & St Anthony School

The Wind

The wind is a howling dog,
A sweeping brush from God,
Brushing leaves from the ground,
The wind brings tidal waves,
And causes erosion in dark caves.
It blows into hurricanes,
But as the sun comes out,
The wind is tamed!

Joseph Harrison (10)
Holy Infant & St Anthony School

Superdog

My dog is a superdog
He does the washing up
He makes the tea
And tidies my room
Well . . . not really!
He'd like to do the washing up
And he'd love to take himself for a walk.

But really he's mad
And he can be quite bad
He chews the clothes
When he gets bored
He likes Jammie Dodgers
And he slavers a lot

But really, I love my non superdog!

Harriet Killeen (10)
Holy Infant & St Anthony School

A Terrible Gloomy Night

The terrible gloomy night was bad
It made everybody in the town feel sad.
Everywhere was very wet
It was the worst weather any town could get.

It was a very bad storm
Not many people felt warm.
There was not a shining moon
The storm would not end soon.

Everywhere was very foggy
And the grass was very soggy.
Even though it's very dark
At least the town had built an ark.

Daniel Groves (9)
Ightenhill Primary School

Lurking In The Dark

Creeping in the dark was a monster
He enters the mystic
It is pitch-black
Beware when you go to bed at night.

He doesn't like the light,
Keep a torch by your bed
Keep your window shut
Beware when you go to bed at night.

Louisa Burrows (9)
Ightenhill Primary School

My Dad Is The Bestest On The Earth

My dad is loving
My dad is kind,
My dad is helpful
My dad is nice.
My dad is funny
At any time.
He is the bestest dad on the Earth
I love him.

Abigail Bowling (8)
Ightenhill Primary School

A Valentine's Poem

Valentine's Day comes every year,
Sometimes early, sometimes late;
It always comes, no matter what,
It comes to say, we care
In every single way.
This is to say I care for you
No matter what you do.
I care so much for you
Upon this special day.

Sarah Bushby (8)
Ightenhill Primary School

What A Wonderful Day

One snowy day
A snowman sits on the lawn,
Footprints cover the ground
The robin makes his clawmarks in the snow,
Children throwing snowballs.
What a wonderful day.

Children going by with their sledges,
Kicking the soft fallen snow,
Their wellies covered in snow.
Snowflakes falling over their heads
I'd come inside if I were you.
What a wonderful day.

Icicles lay on the rocks
Such a pretty sight.
As the children play outside,
May joy come through this snowy day.
What a wonderful day.

Lydia Fairclough (9)
Ightenhill Primary School

What Is Love?

Love is trust
Love is caring
Love is friendship
Love is sharing
Someone loves me and someone loves you.

Everyone has a soulmate
Even me and you
You might have found yours
But I have not
One day I will find him
Someone is out there for me and you
I'll care for him. Will he care for me?

Charlotte Sanders (8)
Ightenhill Primary School

Zombie Catching

A magical mystical gloomy night,
Two fluffy pink monsters grabbed my leg.

Owls lost their sight,
Down came a flying goblin, slowly.

Five little men gave me a fright,
Smaller, smaller, smaller they got,
But the last was a dot.

Up rose the dead with a glance around,
With a flash of light a zombie appeared.

There was a screech of a door,
But no it can't have been!
A dream.

Heather Clements (8)
Ightenhill Primary School

My Family

She has brown hair,
She has blue eyes.
I love her
She loves me.
She is kind
She is helpful,
She is so so nice
She is my mum.

He has black hair,
He has blue eyes.
I love him
He loves me,
He shouts very loud
He thinks he's slim.
He thinks he's strong
He is my dad.

Jack Heyworth (8)
Ightenhill Primary School

In The Cemetery

At night when the clock strikes twelve,
The dead rise from their graves.
Dracular appears with maggots on his face.

The mummies grunt and groan,
Then I hear a moan.
So now it's terror time
The dead bodies commit a crime.

Now the clock strikes one
Everything will be gone,
It's out of sight but lurking underground,
Waiting until the clock strikes midnight.

Stephen Rostron (8)
Ightenhill Primary School

Snowy Days

As the icicles get covered in snow,
As the robin hops along,
As my soaking clothes trail along
As I just walk through the door.
As I blow my drink with a soft blow
As my Maltesers bob up and down,
As my soaking clothes dry,
As the chocolate melts.
As I sit on the carpet, which feels like velvet,
As the frostbite goes away, hour by hour.
As the flames blaze in the fire,
As I drift dreamily away, sleeping silently.

Chloe Colton (9)
Ightenhill Primary School

The Shining Star

One cold windy night
An angel appeared and gave me a fright.
She said, 'I've travelled from afar
To bring you a shining star.

This star will glimmer
It will make you shimmer,
And has a surprise in store for you
It will make your wish come true.'

Take a stroke of this star
It will take you to lands afar
There you'll see your lover boy
And you will have lots of joy.

Adele Morrell (8)
Ightenhill Primary School

Snowy Night

One snowy night, just an ordinary night,
It started to snow at a very ordinary time.
The time was seven o'clock,
The snow started to fall faster.
The snowflakes started to get bigger,
Till they were the size of tennis balls.
The town was covered with deep, deep snow.
But suddenly it stopped,
The rain came down and
The snow was gone.

Jack Green (9)
Ightenhill Primary School

One Dark Night

One dark night in a gloomy street,
A girl walked past to whom she'll meet.
A shining star, a gloomy moon,
And hope that she'll meet you soon.

Round the corner, she sees a sight,
Lots of people and a very bright light.
She sees her friend in the crowded place,
And runs to give her a warm embrace.

Lucy Victoria Davis (9)
Ightenhill Primary School

Seasons

As spring comes into action,
The flowers look up to the sun,
Best time of the year, summer and spring.
But winter is cold and gloomy,
With spring, different to autumn.
Spring is a lot sunnier than the brightest bulb,
And the clock is ticking away,
We don't have much time before we fall.

Luke Stephenson (8)
Nether Kellet Community Primary School

Polly Parrot

Polly parrot sang all day,
Couldn't keep a song away,
And one sad day, a tragedy
A bomb hit Polly, fatally.
She had one warning,
Boom, bang, boom,
Sang her head off -
La! La! Bang!

Danielle Simpson (7)
Nether Kellet Community Primary School

Sweet Honey

I was so pleased when I got Honey, my hamster,
The very best Christmas present ever.
She's so cuddly and cute with her long, twitchy whiskers,
I could play with her forever and ever.
I like watching her playing in the sand,
And when she curls up in my hand
Giving her lots of treats, like apples and carrots and nuts.
But most of all, she likes pod peas and stuffs them in her pouch.
We buy her little things to play with,
Like ladders and tunnels and slides
And when she gets tired from playing,
She goes into her house to hide.

Danielle Watts (9)
Nether Kellet Community Primary School

I Want A Cat Not A Dog

I want a cat not a dog,
Cats are fluffy
Dogs are scruffy,
Cats go miaow
Dogs go woof, woof.
I want a cat not a dog,
But I want a rabbit and a cat!
What should I pick?
Help me out -
I will get both, I think.

Lydia Cowell (7)
Nether Kellet Community Primary School

Motherhood

M otherhood is a difficult time with children
O ther mothers are different, some are hard, some are soft
T hey are sometimes *strict* but some will do anything
H elp is at hand with mums, I wish
E very mum is cool or hot
R ights and wrongs has every mother
H oods are upon your head, when it's raining
O h and healthy food with mothers
O ccasionally Burger King, KFC and McDonalds
D eary me, I know all about motherhood.

Elanor Brown (9)
Nether Kellet Community Primary School

Man's Best Friend

Walking along as she sniffs in the grass
In the river, the ducks slowly pass,
Down flies a heron to catch a trout,
Out of the ground, the flowers sprout.
She spots a sheep and sets off to run,
Hold the lead tightly and spoil her fun.
On the bank the fisherman stand,
While people walk past, hand in hand.

The bridge ahead is small and old
The water below is very cold,
She doesn't care she just jumps in.
The fishermen think it's a sin.
Out she comes, all wet and smelly,
Then she shakes and wobbles her belly.
Becoming tired, she's getting slow,
Time for home, we'd better go.

Joseph Birtwell (11)
Our Lady & St Hubert's RC Primary School

Why Does Rain Evaporate?

Why does rain evaporate?
Why do robbers steal things?
How come birds can fly?
What do we do when we die?

Who made the Earth?
What is the meaning of life?
Why do we go up to space in a rocket?
Who invented the pocket?

Where is Heaven?
Why do people seize land?
What came first, the chicken or the egg?
Why do beggars beg?
Why?

Oliver Woodall (9)
Our Lady & St Hubert's RC Primary School

Chewy Gooey Sweets

I like sweets, they're soft and chewy,
Sometimes they're really gooey.
Out of the packet, here it comes,
Into my mouth, not my mum's.
When I'm really bad,
I have to give one to my dad.
Now it's all mine, all mine, all mine.
Nobody else's, just mine, just mine.
Twisting and twirling, around and around,
Be careful, I might drop it on the ground.
Now it's gone, gone away,
I'll have to find one, another day.

Bethany Hargreaves (11)
Our Lady & St Hubert's RC Primary School

My Granny Is . . .

My granny is a Siamese twin
My granny is as smelly as a bin
My granny has a big fat belly
And the skin on her face wobbles like jelly.
My granny is a pro pop star
My granny's got an old rubbishy car
My granny is a weird belly dancer
She jumps in the air like Rudolf and Prancer
My granny's a star - an old Spice Girl
She makes all the crowd shout and whirl
My granny has an old brown bag
She needs some horrid glasses to
Read her daily mag.
She's as silly as a frying pan
But I still think she's the world's best gran.

Jessica Coy (11)
Our Lady & St Hubert's RC Primary School

My Football Feet

My magic feet
My magic toes
I kick the ball
And in it goes!

I run quite fast
Like a forceful blast
I get the ball
And in it goes!

Into a tackle
My legs crackle
I shoot the ball
And in it goes!

Charleigh Dunn (10)
Our Lady & St Hubert's RC Primary School

My Granny Is A Professor

My granny is a professor
She's got grotty green hair,
She's never been to a hairdresser
And she's got a manic stare.

She always wears a doctor's coat
And she's full of nasty smells,
It gives me a bad, sore throat
What is she up to? She never tells.

She has a secret workspace
That's always dark and scary
She tries to kiss me on the face
But her nose is dark and hairy,

One day she came out to show
She'd mutated two new heads
Which made me scream and shout
So I hid under the bed!

Hannah Parker (11)
Our Lady & St Hubert's RC Primary School

Monkey Poem

Down in the jungle, up in the trees,
Nothing is moving, not even a breeze.
Out pops the head of a mischievous monkey
Stringy and bendy, his limbs are so funky.

Up in the trees, they chitter and chatter
Stepping on sticks, they hear me and scatter.
In the shelter, they play hide-and-seek
Their skill and balance are so unique.

To swing from tree to tree with such effortless ease
They always find someone or something to tease.
In the jungle, they're on their best guard
For perilous predators will pounce on them hard.

Dominic Hogan (11)
Our Lady & St Hubert's RC Primary School

Dolphin

The sea is calm, the sky is clear
And a group of fish are bathing near
They dart about, like silver planes
Organising themselves in silver lanes
And a shape flips, far away
Coming for food, not here to stay
Racing along, a streamlined greyish shape
Makes the wavy surface break.
The dolphin leaps into the air
Aiming for the fish, swimming under there.
The fish, all separate, shoot and swim
As the dolphins start to close in.
Their mouths open, their teeth snap
At last the fish see the deadly trap.
But now they're caught - they have to give up
And they are swallowed in a hungry gulp.
So now the dolphins dive away
Looking for some other prey.
The turquoise sea splashes at their fins
As yet another hunt begins.
And the dolphins splash against the orange sun
Knowing their prey can neither hide nor run.

Hannah Sharkey (10)
Our Lady & St Hubert's RC Primary School

Winter

Snow is falling
Winter has come,
Children dress warmly
Having great fun.

Hurling frozen balls
Of ice and snow,
Who will it hit?
Nobody knows.

Linden Smith (10)
Our Lady & St Hubert's RC Primary School

Monkey Business

Mischievous and playful,
Wild and free,
I'm a monkey that leaps
From tree to tree.
In the leaves,
It's so much fun,
But it's time for bed
When night has begun.
It's dark and damp
All is quiet and still,
But there are predators,
Waiting in the chill.

Morning comes,
It's warm and sunny,
'Time to get food,'
Says Daddy and Mummy.
When Mummy's not there
We play in the sun,
But sometimes we wish
Our parents weren't gone.

In the afternoon,
No one is around,
So we play hide-and-seek,
And wait to be found.
Being a monkey is fun
Because we can be free,
And hopefully no one
Will chop down our tree.

Charlotte Mulcahy (11)
Our Lady & St Hubert's RC Primary School

My Granny

My granny is great
My granny is good,
She treats me nicely
Just like you should.

She tells funny stories
Of life, long ago.
Was she ever like me?
How will I know?

Kane Moreton (10)
Our Lady & St Hubert's RC Primary School

The Roller Coaster

Up, up, the roller coaster goes
Twisting and turning like a wiggly hose
The very first carriage is almost at the top
People screaming at the sight of the drop
Down, down the roller coaster plummets
Wishing it were safely back on the summit
Slower, slower, the roller coaster brakes
Back to the archway above the gates.

Sam Hoole (10)
Our Lady & St Hubert's RC Primary School

Unfit To Be Human?

H orrible looking organs
U nderneath your layers of skin,
M icro-organisms invading people's bodies
A bdominal muscles not working properly
N othing they do for exercise will keep them fit
S illy people can't even take care of themselves.

Tobin Joseph (9)
Our Lady & St Hubert's RC Primary School

No Song To Sing

He has a long neck
And brown polkadots
And if you saw him
You'd shout, 'Great Scot!'
He's a very bright yellow
As well as a strange fellow
He has a big long tongue
But doesn't have a song.

John Parker (10)
Our Lady & St Hubert's RC Primary School

I Wonder

I wonder if the sky could be green?
I wonder if I couldn't be seen?
I wonder if the sun could be blue?
I wonder if sheep could say moo?
I wonder if a pen could write by itself?
I wonder if everyone could have wealth?
I wonder why, I wonder?

Luke Parker (11)
Our Lady & St Hubert's RC Primary School

My Dog

I like my dog, she's dark brown,
Sometimes she looks like she's feeling down.
When she's happy, she plays with her sister Meg,
Then after that, she gets to chew on a postman's leg.

Henry Nazareth-Kay (11)
Our Lady & St Hubert's RC Primary School

Imagine

When I was young I used to think
So many silly things,
Like there were dragons in the sky
And people could grow wings.

I used to watch a tree outside,
Waiting for a fairy.
But all I saw around that tree
Was a dog, so very hairy.

I thought I saw a wicked witch
Flying upon her broom,
Later on, I saw some elves,
Dancing around my room.

Now that I'm a little older,
Those dreams have gone away,
But still I haven't given up hope
That I'll see those creatures one day.

Georgina Wallace (11)
Our Lady & St Hubert's RC Primary School

What Would Happen?

What would happen if everyone was blue?
We wouldn't know who was who!

What would happen if we never died?
What if things happened but we never tried?

What would happen if we never saw the sun?
What would happen if we couldn't run?

What would happen if we didn't have TV?
We wouldn't be able to watch CBBC.

What would happen if girls were boys?
And we all liked different toys.

Phillipa Lees (9)
Our Lady & St Hubert's RC Primary School

Roller Coaster

A scary ride starts off slow
Ready? Here we go!
Up very high
Almost touching the sky.
Facing a slope,
Get a lump in your throat.
Looking down the other side,
People and rides go rushing by
The rest of the fairground, is just a blur,
Do you think they really care?

Begin again, nice and slow,
It seems like you're going low.
In the distance, can they see?
A huge slope staring at me.
Knowing what's coming, they close their eyes,
Down the other side, people screaming,
Tourists staring eyes are beaming.
All of a sudden, they're going slow
But the next band of people are raring to go.

Alice Bradley (10)
Our Lady & St Hubert's RC Primary School

Cinderella

Once upon a long, long time
Comes the story of this rhyme
Cinderella all alone
Lived with ugly sisters in their home.
Had no mum
No hand on head
But she had an evil stepmother instead.
They worked her day and worked her night
And the voice of the sisters was a fright
But 'Phew!' she says. She doesn't really care
If her stepmother and sisters are 'rare'.
But one day, they got some mail
About a prince, who was for sale.
'Oh, it is for a royal ball.'
Said the prince's butler, fat and tall.
'Oh cool,' the sisters said.
But Cinderella was filled with dread.
'Oh you're not going to the ball,
That's the nonsense, nonsense of all.'
Cinderella cried and cried
Until she saw a little light,
It turned into a little lady
'Oh this must be the tax lady,
This is all I've got, here's a tuppence.'
'Oh no, I'm not the tax lady,
I'm a little bit shady
But there's nothing to fear
Your godmother's here.
Of course I'm a fairy
I know I look a bit scary
But I'm just a fairy.
What's wrong?
Do you want a song?'
'No!' said Cinderella,
'I want to dance with that royal fella.
And go to that ball.
Oh that wish is small.
Give me a dress
For my interest

And with a coach of course,
With footman and a horse.
So I shall go to the ball.'
'That wish is big,
Now let me think
Yes done!
Oh, what fun that was.
Now go, the spell goes at 12 o'clock,
So go and have fun in your fancy frock.'
So Cinderella danced and danced
But she didn't really get a chance
To look into the prince's eyes.
Oh of course, the prince was very nice
But when midnight came
There was a fright,
As she went outside
The coach was gone.
Just nothing, nothing!
But when she got back
Nothing intact
As the stepmother shouted
And Cinderella pouted.
But the prince remembered
That there was the shoe
She'd left in the loo.
He said he would find
The girl in his mind.
So he searched the land
On his command
And found Cinderella of course.
So in laughter -
They lived happily ever after.

Elaine Harrison (8)
Out Rawcliffe CE School

Goldilocks And The Three Bears

One day little Goldilocks stood
In the middle of a wood.
There she was and there she saw
A tiny cottage with a great big door.
She then shouted, 'May I come in.'
(She made a great big din)
So she went in all by herself
And there upon the shelf
Were three bowls of porridge, one medium, one small,
Another one, the biggest of all.
She tried the first one, much too hot
So she went to the next porridge pot.
Goldilocks, being quite bold
Tried the next bowl, much to cold.
After horrid porridge Goldilocks felt white
But tried the third bowl, it was just right.
After she had had her fill,
Goldilocks felt rather ill.
She thought she needed a sit down
So she had a look around.
There she found some chairs,
Not knowing they belonged to bears.
'I might try this one,' she said with a frown,
'But if I get up, I may never get down.
'I think I'll go for a lower chair,
How about that one over there.'
She tried the next chair, much too wide
She could not reach from side to side.
The next chair was a perfect fit
But as soon as she sat on it
The chair suddenly began to break.
She knew she'd made a big mistake.
As soon as she'd picked herself off the floor
Got up again, ran headlong to the door
But then she said,
'I think I'll have a rest in bed.'
First was too hard, second too soft,
Goldilocks felt so ill she coughed
But the next bed was just right
So instead of feeling white

Goldilocks felt sleeping was the knack
She didn't know the bears were back.
Baby Bear screamed and said,
'Someone's eaten my porridge, and now she's asleep in my bed.'
Then Goldilocks ran away
And still to this day
She promises never to go
Back to the woods where bears roam.

Kate Cornthwaite (8)
Out Rawcliffe CE School

Space Is Marvellous

S pace is wonderful, I'd like to see the stars,
    I'd look out of the window and maybe I'd see Mars.
P lease let me go up there, I'd like to see the planets,
    But if I met an alien, I'm sure I'd shake and panic.
A stronauts are clever, astronauts are smart,
    Astronauts drive around in a fancy space cart.
C omets go flying by my window and light up the dark sky.
E veryone should be an astronaut sharing this experience,
    Seeing all the planets and the difference.

Simon Dewsnip (8)
St Joseph's RC Primary School, Calderdale

The Sun

The sun is bright it, shines so light.
When it goes down it is out of sight.
The sun has got lots of might,
The sun bites if it doesn't like the sight.
We all said, 'Night-night, sleep tight.'

Laura McDade (8)
St Joseph's RC Primary School, Calderdale

Silver

Tonight is Bonfire Night
I am going to the beach,
To let them go and join
The stars.

I wake up and look in my mirror,
Then I open my curtains.
I see the waves crashing
Against the silver rocks.

Next I get dressed and
Put a silver chain around
My cold neck, I'm scared.
Scared I'm going to die.

I go down the stairs,
I see our silver coat rack
Swinging, death is coming.
I will regret going on the beach.

I eat breakfast with my silver spoon,
Then I eat lunch and tea.
I'm going to the beach,
It's dark, the car jolts to a stop.

I open the door and get out,
It's cold, I find a silver penny,
I pick it up and walk onto the sand,
Then I lose them, my whole family.

I can no longer hear them,
Just the sound of the waves
In the far distance. I shiver,
And walk, shiver and walk.

Then I slip, I'm falling.
I stop all of a sudden,
My eyes slowly close,
The last thing I see is my chain.

I am dangling and with that
I die in moonlight and fireworks.
I regret wearing my chain,
It has brought me bad luck.

But It will always stay silver.

Anna Brannigan (10)
St Joseph's RC Primary School, Calderdale

Gold

In the heart of the gold, shimmering desert,
Is the amazing soft silky sand,
And when a toe touches it you feel relaxed,
In the gold desert.

Gold is the flash of light,
The flash that is so blinding,
The flash as beautiful as a gold ring
In the flash of gold.

Gold is a soothing colour.

Melissa Barker (10)
St Joseph's RC Primary School, Calderdale

Brum Oily Go

G o they shout!
R oar they go round the corner,
A nd what's that? Oh he's collided!
N o he's out!
D ancing and singing on the podium.

P lease don't crash
R ound the bend they screech
I n the pits they go!
X tra fuel please.

Holly Howorth (11)
St Joseph's RC Primary School, Calderdale

Running Through A Forest

Running through a forest
fooling squelchy mud under my toes.
Seeing trees grown high over me.
It's my secret place to go,
I find a clear blue river
To swim in and to play.
I can hear the waterfall
as the far wild horses neigh.
The cold air stings my face in joy
as I see the trees look jealous and groan.
I can taste spring water in the back of my mouth.
I am in a secretive zone,
I find that the animals trust me.
I can see every animal in sight,
they all jump in the pool and play with me
and we are going to play all night.

Charlie Kane (10)
St Joseph's RC Primary School, Calderdale

Sock Drawer

I live in a dark place.
In this drawer there is no space.
For another sock to be put with me
I am odd, it is easy to see.

The others laugh because they are pairs,
The boy takes them out because his feet are bare.
His feet are cold, they smell of sweat,
The socks will be soaking because his feet are so wet.

Callum Hall (10)
St Joseph's RC Primary School, Calderdale

Calculators

Calculators, calculators
Working out sums in one
Knowing all the answers
Until their batteries are gone.

Calculators are like mini minds
Hard-working and reliable
But if you use them for cheating
You get in lots of trouble.

My teacher says you should not use them
Because they are cheating
But one night as I passed the school
She was using one at a meeting.

Kelly Collier (11)
St Joseph's RC Primary School, Calderdale

The Dusty Old Mirror

I am dusty and covered in cobwebs,
I am lonely and scared of these walls.
I am stuck with a reflection of dust,
I am only just hanging because of my string.
I get lots of fingerprints on my dusty screen.

I listen to the chatter of the little spiders,
I am laughed at by the flies flying round.
I am old and need a clean,
I am sick of the same old scene,
So take me back to the old days.

James Frain (11)
St Joseph's RC Primary School, Calderdale

My Cat

I have a fluffy cat,
he's smooth and soft
and he's *not* fat.

My cat is brown, black and white.
When he jumps
he uses all his might.

My cat has long, sharp claws
and you can see his sharp teeth
when he opens his jaws.

As you might already know
my cat is always jumping,
scratching and biting
and that's why my cat's
called *Scratch.*

Anna Barlow (10)
St Peter's CE School, Bury

Friends

I have lots of friends,
but they all have different ends.
Sometimes we fight,
but we never bite.
When we play games,
we make lots of silly names.
When they sleep at mine,
we stay up all the time,
those funny friends of mine.

Colette Dickinson (10)
St Peter's CE School, Bury

My Cat Romeo

Romeo, Romeo is the best
He is better than the rest
He's furry and cute, also small
Romeo's got strong legs and feet to break his fall.
A rough tongue
A tail quite long
Romeo, Romeo lapping up milk
His gorgeous fur
It feels like silk.
Oh Romeo, Romeo he's the best little cat
All the prize-winning cats, he's better than that
Romeo is black and white
He's top cat on the street, he always wins the fight.
We're always together Romeo and me
I love him lots, can't you see!

Melissa Porter (10)
St Peter's CE School, Bury

Seasons

Winter is fun in the snow
and it is mad
playing in the snow
but best of all is
Christmas.

Autumn is cold,
very, very cold.
It has lots of crunchy leaves
and conkers
and all the other stuff.

Spring is fun,
very, very fun.
The fun lambs
the buds,
the flower buds.

Summer is hot
very, very hot.
Splashing in the sea
with my friend
and me.

Jay Thornley (11)
St Peter's CE School, Bury

Teachers

T eachers are kind and funny
E nd of the day they are hungry
A fter school they mark our work
C hecking it all, alert, alert!
H appy faces all around
E nd of the day homework surrounding
R ight on time, school in the morning.

Cara-Lee Atkinson (9)
St Peter's CE School, Bury

Friends

F is for friends I think everyone has got
R is for realising that everyone has got a best mate
I is for intelligent friends and very pretty
E is for everyone I hang around with
N is for nasty mates I don't think I've got
D is for my dear friends.

Gemma Harkin (10)
St Peter's CE School, Bury

Weather

The rain is such a pain
Because everybody complains.
The sun is just beautiful,
The snow is cold
But it's good to hold.
The weather is better,
There's so much more.

Mark McGlynn (10)
St Peter's CE School, Bury

Love

Love, love here and there,
It is never to scare,
When people sing and dance,
They send messages
And it is beautiful
And is cute.
It sounds like a heart beating
It is beating badly and mad
It is also good.
People kissing each other
And hugging and sending love messages.
They send romantic things.

Chelsea Barry (10)
St Peter's CE School, Bury

Birds

B is for birds that fly all day long
 I is for independent birds that fly alone
R is for robins that fly in winter
D is for a dove, a kind of bird
S is for seagulls that fly by the seaside.

Declan Kerr (10)
St Peter's CE School, Bury

Beckham The Star

Beckham, Beckham, he is very posh
taking corners and bending them across.
Beckham, Beckham running up the wing
all the away fans thinking it's a dream.

Adam Dawson (11)
St Peter's CE School, Bury

My Best Friend

My best friend is called Nicole Shortt,
She has eyes that look like blue, shining marbles,
She has rosy red lips
And she hates apple pips.
She has ginger hair,
And is always fair.
She is a good laugh
And loves to have a bath.
She has rosy red cheeks,
Her worst vegetables are leeks.
She is really kind
And always in mind
And that is my best friend,
Nicole Shortt!

Michelle Morris (10)
St Peter's CE School, Bury

Manchester United

Manchester United are the best,
even better than the rest!

Old Trafford the best ground,
you have to pay to enter.
A pound is not enough.

But you're missing about
ten goals a game,
so ask your mum to give you money,
don't be such a pain.

Liverpool, Arsenal, City aren't the correct team,
United beat Arsenal, a hat-trick by Keane.

Connor Stansfield (10)
St Peter's CE School, Bury

Kittens

Kittens, kittens
I love them
sleeping on the sofa
so cosy and warm.
With their eyes closed
That's what I like
about them
for one.

Kittens, kittens
like eating a lot
jumping on the sides
eating the meat
that all the family
were going to eat
for their tea.

Kittens, kittens
are so cute
sitting on my lap
making you uncomfy
and making them comfy
and making a very loud
purring sound.
Purr, purr, purr, purr.

Kittens, kittens
biting your toes
and scratching you
on your arms and legs
and playing with
your string.

Rebecca Torr (9)
St Peter's CE School, Bury

On The Cover Of My Diary

On the cover of my diary just the other day
I wrote the sort of message to keep my mum away
Snoopers watch out or . . . so I wrote
Please take notice of this note
Keep away just get lost
Or else I'll call Inspector Frost
Do not try to sneak a look
Inside this precious book
Do not stay please just go
Or you might learn what you don't want to know!

Danielle Marshall (10)
St Peter's CE School, Bury

Snow Is . . .

Snow is a sparkling carpet
Snow is a screwed up ball in a bin
Snow is a football kicked in the sky
Snow is a button dropped down a drain
Snow is a crystal on the floor
Snow is blobs of paint
Snow is pompoms in the air.

Jake Patton (10)
St Stephen's CE Primary School, Bury

My Dad's Car

My dad's car is so squeaky
It's bumpy down the road
The engine stalls the tyres pop
My dad screams, 'It's really old.'
He goes and buys a new one
He drives it out the drive
He goes to bed to rest his head
He says his car's the best!

Billy Jones (10)
St Stephen's CE Primary School, Bury

Down By The Sea

The trees like dancers moving in the wind
The smoke rising as the candle flickered and dimmed.

The waves are crashing up against the rocks
Time is wasted as the clock ticks and tocks.

The sun is shining high in the sky
The sun is setting, the babies cry.

Natalie Walker (11)
St Stephen's CE Primary School, Bury

Spring Morning

The morning shines
The bird song rhymes.
Clouds drift
The birds are swift.
The grass rustles in the breeze
The pollen makes you sneeze.
The field mouse does run
Playing in the sun.
Rabbits hop
Some bop.
The deer protect their young from danger
There's a wolf but no ranger.
The deer run away . . .
The wolf decides not to stay.
The night comes
Hear the drums.
It's gone dark
Hear the lark.
It's gone chilly
The badgers play silly.
The wolves sneak
Then they have a peek.
It's the day the wolf got his prey
Some of the rabbits are still grey.
It has turned dawn
A doe had a fawn
Love is all around
We're all lying on the ground.
Night, night little fawn on the floor
I want to play more.

Shannon Booth (10)
St Stephen's CE Primary School, Bury

Louis Saha

Saha, Saha, Saha,
Is Man U's best star,
He scores a goal,
Better than Andy Cole's,
He's got braids in his hair,
Which it seems is fair.
He used to play for Fulham,
Man U bought him for £12 million,
But should have been priced at £12 billion.
Also my mum says he's *brilliant!*

Ben Howarth (11)
St Stephen's CE Primary School, Bury

My Dog

A fast runner
A lazy lump
A large eater
A quiet yawner
A playful thing
A child biter
A furry fellow
A cat chaser
A big barker
My best pet.

Steven Taylor (10)
St Stephen's CE Primary School, Bury

My Imaginary Best Friend

A smarty pants
A girly sort
A golden girl
A gorgeous babe
A pretty chick
A laughing monkey
A secret teller
A dancing queen
A singing princess
An ice cream addict.

Iqra Mahmood (10)
St Stephen's CE Primary School, Bury

Christmas

A snow dog
A snowy beard
A large reindeer
A snow world
A wet Christmas
A snowman
A red Christmas
A slippy ice
An ice age
A Christmas dinner.

Sam Fitzpatrick (10)
St Stephen's CE Primary School, Bury

In The War

In the war	Bombs are flying
People died,	Sounds of guns
No one swore	Parents are crying
But they could lie	Because of their sons

So don't step out of your door
You'll get knocked down on the floor,

because . . .

People are guarding,
Armies are charging,
On the day of the Second World War.

Natasha Tyrie (10)
St Stephen's CE Primary School, Bury

The Wise Men

On a long journey the wise men went,
With gold, myrrh and frankincense.
They travelled far, high and low,
But then they didn't know where to go
And suddenly they saw a really bright light
They all thought it was an incredible sight.
Following the star they met Herod
And then they all shook with terror.
At last they finally reached the stable,
The newborn king was lying in the cradle.

Abigail Kitchen (11)
St Stephen's CE Primary School, Bury

A Fierce Battle

To battle for the king they ride,
soldiers and weapons side by side,
to defeat the fire beast with spear and blade,
but the soldiers' lives will probably fade.

Three hours passed, the dragon slain,
but on the floor lay men in pain.

Armour pierced from a fierce battle,
now we return back to the great castle.

Jake Dolsey (11)
St Stephen's CE Primary School, Bury

Girl Pie

A beautiful, intelligent girl
A giggleful of rose-scented bubbles
A gossipful of gold crystal earrings
A kiss of sparkly lipstick
A bottleful of slimy, sludgy hair gel
A sneeze of white sprinkly talcum powder
One pie dish.

Method:
Place the girl on the pie dish
Put soap in her mouth
Stick earrings in her hair
Paint nail varnish all over her
Mix the hair gel and talcum powder together
Then pour on top
Cook till Sunday.

James Cummings (8)
St Thomas' CE Primary School, Lytham St Annes

Girlie Pie

A strong sniff of dandelion perfume
A thick, bumpy layer of plum-coloured icing.
A murder of claret lipstick
One perfect groovy chick diary.
A few soft fluffy teddies to line the bottom
Three million bars of soft, gooey apple soap.
Five small, tight, silky dresses
Far too much sparkling gold glitter
A litter of six fluffy white kittens.

Liam Bloor (7)
St Thomas' CE Primary School, Lytham St Annes

May

The month of May
Which in every day
Is full of joy
When flowers bloom
There is no gloom.

You can catch butterflies
When winter dies
No rain, no clouds
But blue skies and sun
So come with us and join the fun

When birds come out
You go on walk about
With sheep in the fields
And the sun in the sky
Let your happiness fly.

The month of May.

Sarah Gillard (10)
St Thomas' CE Primary School, Barrowford

Untitled

I'm a little pink fish
With quite a big tail
I always wish
That I could be a whale

I have a big smile
Sneaky little eyes
It takes me a while
To catch tiny green flies

I have small bent fins
Rosy-red cheeks
I eat my food in tiny tins
I'm often scared of big yellow beaks.

Becky Nolan (10)
St Thomas' CE Primary School, Barrowford

Untitled

In the big and lonely mountains
There's waterfalls not fountains
You'll never find a single bear.
A pack of wolves is all that's there
You can hear them howling through the night
Four grey, two black and one white
The grass that grows on the mountain bottom
Is more than twice as soft as cotton
It's what they live off, what they eat
Twice as tasty, better than meat
They're the only animals there
So they have to be vegetarians.

Helena Chadwick (9)
St Thomas' CE Primary School, Barrowford

My Annoying Sister

I've got a sister who's very pretty,
She's kind and giving and always witty.
But we went on holiday to a Spanish villa,
She got so annoying I wanted to kill her.
Her and her friend stole all my dresses
She used them to make lots of messes.
So in return I picked her locks
Then I stole all their knickers and socks!

Daisy Stinchon (10)
St Thomas' CE Primary School, Barrowford

When I Went

When I went to the zoo,
My brother went to the loo,
He found a fat cat,
Eating a rat
And he swelled up like a balloon.

Ruth Hallows (10)
St Thomas' CE Primary School, Barrowford

Stars

The midnight sky is clear,
Until little stars appear,
Dashing through the sky,
So quick it caught your eye.

You can tell a secret,
Don't worry it won't tell,
A star is just like magic,
Casting a spell.

Samantha Caraher (10)
St Thomas' CE Primary School, Barrowford

Puppy Love

(Sung to 'Bobby Shaftoe')

Feater Packer he loves Fee,
But she chases Manny Lee,
Manny says that he loves me,
Poor old Feater Packer.

Feater Packer's not too clever,
Fee says she will love him never,
He says he'll love Fee forever,
Potty Feater Packer.

Manny Lee is chasing Fee now,
Fee has gone off Manny Lee now,
Feater Packer's after me now,
Perfect Feater Packer!

Kate Webster (9)
St Thomas' CE Primary School, Barrowford

Boring

It's boring at school,
Boring! Boring!
I don't want to go cos it's
Boring! Boring!

Volume in maths,
Boring! Boring!
Poetry in literacy,
Boring! Boring!
Mountains in geography,
Boring! Boring!

Electricity in science,
Boring! Boring!
World War II in history,
Boring! Boring!
But art and DT
Hooray!

Ammaarah Patel (10)
The Valley Community School

Teachers

T eachers are sometimes strict with the badly behaved students,
E xtremely clever to teach the class,
A nd they always hope their students will get level 5s,
C hallenging work given by the teachers,
H oping that she gives us stars for good work,
E very student has a favourite teacher,
R emember mine is Mrs Barnard and Mrs Musa,
S econdary school I'm ready for harder work!

Bilal Patel (11)
The Valley Community School

Rugby

Rugby is a sport for boys,
But not for the people who play with toys,
It is a rough and tough game,
But you don't call each other names,
If you release your fury,
There will be lots of injury,
Touch the ground with the ball,
But never think you're small,
Always think you're strong,
And always get along.

Ashraf Patel (11)
The Valley Community School

Rain

The rain splashes and dashes and clashes,
The rain falls like diamonds and crystals,
It falls like stars.

The rain glimmers and shimmers and flickers and sparkles,
And gleams like glass,
Beaming and glistening and rising.

Irfan Patel (10)
The Valley Community School

The Thunder!

The lightning clashes and flashes and crashes and glares,
It lightens like a laser,
And stares like a lion.

The thunder is deafening and ear-splitting and piercing and blaring,
The thunder banging as loud as fireworks,
Shrieking like a ghost.

Weseema Patel (11)
The Valley Community School

Nature

Nature, nature all around,
These are the things that I have found,
There's squirrels and nuts, leaves on trees,
Flowers and plants and busy bees,
I can hear water trickling nearby,
The birds twittering way up high,
The weather changes all the time,
It could be bad or could be fine.
Fishes are swimming all day,
New tadpoles are born during May.
In silence the animals sleep at night,
When the stars come out and shine bright.

Aameena Mohammed (10)
The Valley Community School

Rain

Rain, rain falling down,
Falling heavily on the ground,
Filling gutters with water,
And making the sky go darker.

Raees Patel (11)
The Valley Community School

Classroom Rules

Don't scrape chairs, don't be late,
Don't be rude, be on time,
Keep in line and be quiet,
Don't shout out and don't call names.

And listen to the teacher
You should do what you are told,
Stop laughing and do some work,
These are the words that the teacher's say,
She says you should follow the classroom rules.

Classroom rules are useful,
They help you stay out of trouble,
If you don't obey these rules,
Your next trip will be to the head teacher's room!

Naushaad Patel (10)
The Valley Community School

Stars

There are stars everywhere,
There are shining stars
And shooting stars,
Stars in the sky shining bright,
That only come out in the night,
There are stars that you stick,
And star lollies that you lick,
Using stars as a template,
Or helping people to find their fate,
Stars as a border,
Or stars as a picture,
There is every kind of star,
In this whole wide world.

Nasira Patel (11)
The Valley Community School

Football

Football is a sport for lads,
Where you wear socks and shin pads,
You take the centre and pass the ball,
You'd never think it would be you at all,
You take the shot and hope to score,
Taking more shots more and more,
Sensational what a goal!
Coming off the big white pole,
Half-time lads!

When the players come out again,
All the fans scream and go insane,
You take the centre and try to shoot,
With your lucky and astonishing boot.
You take a shot,
Oh what a pot,
In the back of the net,
That the keeper will regret,
Full time lads!

Mohamed Bhaiji (11)
The Valley Community School

Friends

F riends are really kind and it is easy to find,
R ace with us and play with us and never make a fuss,
I 'm in trouble and he comes to help -
    and when you are sitting in a car,
        he tells you to wear your belt.
E xtremely kind and clever, but when it's time to do homework,
    He says 'Call me later.'
N ever swears and never calls names, and plays fantastic games,
D o the things which are not bad that your friend tells you to do,
    and also listen to your parents too!
S hezhad my friend is like a brother to me.

Suhail Mahomed (11)
The Valley Community School

Friends

Friends support
Me when in trouble
A friend in need is a friend indeed,
Friends are like family,
Friends are kind,
Friends are thoughtful,
Friends are helpful,
Friends are also generous,
Friends are the best.

Amin Adam (10)
The Valley Community School

Bolton School

I am applying for Bolton School,
I hear there is good education,
I studied hard to pass the exam,
And that's what I did, I passed just in time,
I was happy just to find out what I had done,
Now I have my interview hard, but easy to do,
I hope I will pass, I am confident,
And if I succeed I will be going this September.

Shajeda Sidda (11)
The Valley Community School

Thunder

T hunder is foreboding!
H ustling quickly the leaves fall down,
U nbelievable weather is everywhere,
N ever go out, the weather is blare,
D oes not stop until the misty night,
E arly people switch on lights,
R ain, rain, everywhere.

Asifali Adam (10)
The Valley Community School

Classroom Rules

Don't scrape chairs and don't be late,
Don't be rude and don't disturb,
Keep in line and keep on time,
Don't shout out and don't run about.

Listen to the teacher,
Do as you are told,
Stop chattering, work,
No laughing and giggling, quiet!
These
    Are
        The classroom
                Rules!

Aysha Bhaloda (11)
The Valley Community School

Bullies

There was a boy,
He was always sad,
He didn't get picked for the team,
The kids at school were so mean.

He didn't feel right,
He cried at night,
He didn't want to go to school,
He wanted to be popular and be really cool.

Then one day he met a girl,
In her hair she had a pearl,
She looked so sweet,
She was perfect, her work is always neat.

Before the weekend the girl said to the boy,
'I don't like those bullies, they know who to annoy,'
Then together they went away,
Now they're cool and the bullies aren't cool,
They can't play.

Lauren Downes
Thorn CP School

Five Little Monsters

Five little monsters,
By the light of the moon,
Stirring pudding, pudding with a
Wooden pudding spoon.
The first one says
'It mustn't be Micky,
That will make me sicky.'
The second one says
'It mustn't be dirty
That will make me thirsty.'
The third one says
'It mustn't be pink,
That will make me wink.'
The forth one says,
'It mustn't be mean that
Will make me keen.'
The fifth one giggles
And hiccups, jumps and hums
To the moon and licks all the
Pudding from the wooden pudding spoon,

Abbey Broadbent (6)
Thorn CP School

Swimming Under The Sea

The dolphin whistled, 'One, two, three,'
Started up the band by swimming in the sea,
The dolphin asked the shark if he'd danced,
The octopus said he'd take a chance,
The crab sang 'Clap, clap, clap, clap'
And all the creatures and a rap.

The sea horse led the conga line
And all the little fish came behind,
And they swam and swam and swam
With all their might and
They swam for the rest of the night.

Jessica Procter (7)
Thorn CP School

That Night

The rain thrashed down upon the stable roof,
The trees made shadows using their branches,
The wind sent a chilling breeze into the air,
This is how it felt on that night!

The clouds seemed to form a great black hole,
The flowers all went off to bed during this time,
The grass made a crunching noise as you stepped on it,
This is how it felt on that night!

The sky began to clear and the sun began to rise,
The deep darkness turned to bright light,
The Earth was awoken once again,
This is how it felt on that morning!

Kayleigh McGuinness (11)
Thorn CP School

Warning!

When I am an old woman,
I shall wear bright pink,
And say words like 'fink' instead of think,
Play my music at the maximum,
With my windows wide open!

I shall go to McDonald's and order a Big Mac,
Wear high-heel boots with pink socks to match.

Whenever I see a grey hair I'll dye it blue,
Just for a dare,
I'll learn how to surf in Australia
And poke people with my stick.

But maybe I ought to practice a little now,
So people who know me are not too shocked or surprised,
When they suddenly see me eating fries.

Cynthia Li (11)
Westholme Middle School

Happiness And Sadness

Happiness is the key to locking sadness in a chest,
It feels like you can relax and let your fears melt
                    away in the hot sun.
It looks like it is your birthday and you have got
                a brand new looking sharp sports car,
It tastes like you are free, no traps and no hard work,
A happy day is when there is no hard work until you get a job.

Sadness is when a fire strikes your home,
Sadness feels like when somebody is killed,
It looks like you are in trouble,
It tastes like you are trapped,
A sad day is when you have lost a fortune.

David Lee (8)
Westholme Middle School

Spring

Sitting in the garden
Looking at flowers
Looking at the pretty sight
For hours and hours.

Watching the daffodils
All in a row
All their little heads
Swishing to and fro.

Primroses and snowdrops
Bluebells that ring
Birds that tweet
And flutter and sing.

All the little birds
And all the pretty flowers
I wish I could stay
For a few more hours.

Rebecca Arton (11)
Westholme Middle School

I Like That Stuff

It's brown, yummy and melts in the sun,
It comes in bars, powder and delicious looking eggs,
Chocolate,
I like that stuff!

It's fluffy and sweet, you can buy it at fairs,
It's sugary, messy and melts in your mouth,
Candyfloss,
I like that stuff!

Bees make it but you can buy it in jars,
It's sticky, sweet and runny,
Honey,
I like that stuff!

It's brown, fizzy and very bubbly,
It tastes great with lemon and ice,
Coke,
I like that stuff!

Sophie Janus (10)
Westholme Middle School

The Witch

The ugly horrible witch
Whose hair did nothing but itch.

Had a face as wrinkly as a prune
And lips a dark shade of maroon.

Her nose was as pointed as a sharp spike
And her teeth as sharp as a pike's.

Her chins were like rolls of black pudding
And her eyes when she cried, started flooding.

The witch had warts by the score
And a voice like an old lion's roar.

But our witch wasn't cruel or unkind
She was as gentle as a witch you could find.

Ruby Kay (10)
Westholme Middle School

The Joyous Light Of Spring

While we are now in darkness
I think of all the light
The flowers and the beauty
It's spring of course - oh the sight!

When I wander through the park
With blossoms on the trees
I see the little ducklings hatch
The awe, the fantasies!

While we are now in darkness
I think of all the light
The flowers and the beauty
It's spring of course - oh the sight!

The flowers circled round the trees
All in a margined line
With different coloured petals
Oh, the wonderful times!

While we are now in darkness
I think of all the light
The flowers and the beauty
It's spring of course - oh the sight!

You see all of these lovely things
Which I appreciate
I wonder if you feel the same
I just hope it doesn't come late!

Hannah MacIntosh (10)
Westholme Middle School

Seasons In Character

I am the spring,
As sweet as fresh dew,
I am cool and refreshing,
And eager for new,
I make new life wherever I go,
I am as pretty as flowers but don't say so!

I am the summer,
I am glowing and warm,
As hot as a fire,
And never forlorn,
My hair tumbles low and touches the Earth,
My smile can beam for all it is worth.

I am the autumn,
I am weary and worn,
My fingers are brittle,
My coat is all torn,
My auburn complexion flows down to the ground,
Another year of my age is turning around.

I am the winter,
I am stubborn and mean,
My fingers are icicles,
You'll know when I've been,
I carpet the Earth with my frost, ice and snow,
I leave chaos and destruction wherever I go!

Megan Hindle (10)
Westholme Middle School

I Like That Stuff

It's chewy, it's gooey,
It's brown, it sticks to your teeth,
Toffee,
I like that stuff!

It's fluffy, it's sticky and it's squashy,
You can get it in lots of colours,
Candyfloss,
I like that stuff!

It's transparent, you can't hold it,
It can be strong, it is in the air,
Wind,
I like that stuff!

It's white, each grain is tiny,
I like it on some of my food,
Salt,
I like that stuff!

Harriet Salvesen-Sawh (9)
Westholme Middle School

Warning - Part 2

When I am old I will wear my PJ's in the rain,
With knee length boots and I wouldn't care,
I will spend my money on a wicked new sports car,
I shall open all my windows and doors in the house,
I will pump the music as loud as I can,
I will buy a motorbike and drive it well over the limit,
And have a wide screen TV,
I shall go to Thorntons and stock up chocolate,
I will visit theme parks and go on all the big fast rides,
I will sneak in through the back door at rock concerts,
And even if bodyguards stop me, I will bat my lashes,
But maybe I should practice being like an old lady now,
Who knows what I might turn out like?

Emily Green (11)
Westholme Middle School

Spring Poem

Gone has the icy winter wind,
'Spring's arrived' the birds all sing,
Flowers are dancing in the air,
Children play without a care,
No snow is falling on the ground,
We listen to the merry spring sound,
Easter eggs are hidden away,
We have to find them on Easter day.

New baby lambs are born today,
Horses eat lots of golden hay,
Me and my friends are playing tig,
Tulips and daffodils are growing big,
Winter's gone, spring is here,
I know that summer's very near.

Rachael Moodie (10)
Westholme Middle School

Spring Poem

When spring comes round every year,
Everyone is filled with cheer,
Daffodils grow and grow,
Finding their way after the snow.

Signs of spring are all around,
Lush green grass grows on the ground,
Joyful lambs leap in the air,
They run round here and there.

The sun shines down so bright and kind,
Warming everyone who it can find,
Springtime is everywhere,
With lots of joy for all to share.

Fiona Blacklidge (11)
Westholme Middle School

Christmas Party

Parents chatting
Children swimming
Dogs snapping
Teenagers kissing.

Mums nagging
Dads betting
People running
Teachers yapping.

Audience clapping
Parents stuffing
Dogs running
Winners winning.

Children clapping
Light scattering
Parents hugging
Dogs puffing.

Children hopping
People rapping
Audience sitting
Children hugging.

Romana Alli (10)
Westholme Middle School

This Drop Of Water

This drop of water on my hand may have been . . .
Anne Frank's tears while writing her diary,
Or a piece of the iceberg that sunk the great Titanic.

This drop of water in my hand may have been . . .
The sweat of a footballer after he scored a goal,
Or the tear of Prince Charles when he heard Princess
Diana had died in a car crash.

This drop of water on my hand may have been . . .
In the grapes that might have been served to Cleopatra,
Or the Vikings' sweat while raiding the monasteries.

This drop of water in my hand may have been . . .
The T-Rex's tears when her baby was being killed,
Or the tears of Rachel Steven after she heard Sclub had split up.

This drop of water on my hand may have been . . .
In a drink made for Gandhi,
Or a drop of sweat from an Egyptian while building a pyramid.

This drop of water in my hand may have been . . .
The sparkling dew off grass of the first morning on Earth,
Or the Romans' sweat whilst fighting Boudicca.

Simone Masterson (9) & Emma Louise Booth (10)
Westholme Middle School

Warning!

When I am an old woman I shall wear bright pink,
I shall read Smash Hits magazine,
And never miss EastEnders or Emmerdale,
I shall poke people with my stick,
And play really loud music,
I shall wear mini skirts and groovy tights,
And wear furry coats in winter,
I shall wear blue and purple eye make-up,
And wear high-heel shoes.
I shall eat loads of samples from shops,
And go to surfing and abseiling classes.
I shall go to Hawaii twice a year,
And learn to hula dance.

Maybe I ought to practise a little now?
So people who know me are not too shocked and surprised,
When suddenly I am old and start to wear bright pink.

Rosie McCann (10)
Westholme Middle School

Give Me A Book

'Give me a book,' said Jack,
'Give me a word,' said Sam,
'Give me a title,' said Pam,
'Give me a library,' said Pam.

'Give me an information book,' said David,
'Give me a pop up picture book,' said Matt,
'Give me a non fiction book,' said Chris,
'Give me a reading book,' said Pat.

'Give me a picture book,' said Michael,
'Give me some concentration,' said Ted,
'Give me fairy tales,' said Myles,
'Give me a monster book,' said Fred.

Jack Bolton (7)
Westholme Middle School

Warning - Part 2

I'm going to be an old woman with a difference,
I'll hog all the slopes and knock down small
                              children with my board,
I'll jump all the black jumps and break all the
                              bones in my body and not care!
I will dance down to Asda at 6am singing
'Sk8ter Boi' at the top of my voice.
I will never sit down to read the paper,
And always wear my ski suit whether hot or cold,
And spend all my pension on an around the world cruise.

I'm going to be an old woman with a difference,
I will go out in the rain in my thongs and strapless bra!
I won't clean the dishes or wash my socks and
Only have a shower once a month,
But maybe I should practice a little now so that
People who know me won't be surprised when
Suddenly I am old and start to jump the black jumps!

Tori Redmond (10)
Westholme Middle School

Springtime Is Near

Springtime is near
So I look outside and peer,
Looking for the signs
At this time of year.

Waiting for lambs to be born
And spring flowers to form,
Icy winds will disappear,
Now that spring is near.

Waiting for the snow to melt
And soon the warm out will be felt,
Blowing through the trees so green,
Soon spring will be seen.

Emily Earnshaw (10)
Westholme Middle School

The Witch Is A Hideous Creature

The witch is a hideous creature,
Whose eyes are like green glowing peas,
Her fingers are as far-reaching as from
Her ugly head to her knobbly knees.

The witch is a hideous creature,
Whose face is covered in festering warts,
Her hair is as knotted as netting,
And she often has evil thoughts.

The witch is a hideous creature,
Whose teeth are as black as coal,
She smells like rotten apples
And that's why no one likes her at all.

The witch is a hideous creature,
Whose clothes are all tattered and torn,
Her tongue is as sharp as a razor,
And she's been like that since she was born.

Vicky Haworth (10)
Westholme Middle School

I Wish I Could Fly

I wish I could fly,
Like a big mosquito catching its prey,
Like a fruit bat collecting fruit,
Like a space shuttle taking off the launch pad,
Like a flying fish diving in the water,
Like a jet zooming through the air.

Matthew Parker (7)
Westholme Middle School

Warning

When I am a grandma I will . . .
Invite a rock band to church and get them
To play the National Anthem.
I will wear stilettos on a rainy day with a
Sparkly boob tube and knickers.
When I am a grandma I will have . . .
Stacks and stacks of shoes that are 3 sizes small,
I will teach my grandchildren to spit and always
Speak slang . . . 'Yo dude'
When I am a grandma I will . . .
Put padding in my bra (3 inches thick)
And dance with a Hoover
I will also wear red lipstick with a beige suit and
Take my grandchildren to school on a motorbike.
When I am a grandma I will have . . .
Thousands of tattoos and plenty of boyfriends,
Don't ask why I'm thinking of this now . . .
I'm only 5!

Alice Singleton (10)
Westholme Middle School

Spring

Spring is here,
How do I know?
The little flowers
Start to grow.

Little chicks
And bunnies play,
Here comes spring
With its brighter days.

Spring is here,
How do I know?
A little lamb
Told me so.

Lucy Shephard (11)
Westholme Middle School

Snowballs

Down falls the snow
Falling on the ground,
Pick it up, roll it in your hands,
Throw it at someone,
Dodge theirs,
Do it again!
Hit them, oh no,
They've hit you.

Patrick McMullan (8)
Whittle-Le-Woods Primary School

The Donkey

The donkey
Is lovely and soft,
He canters around
When he walks and his
Feet go clip-clop,
His feet are as hard as rock,
When he eats, he goes munch,
The lovely donkey.

Shannon Touhey (8)
Whittle-Le-Woods Primary School

The Snow Rhyme

I like the way the snow crunches and slushes,
I like the way you pick it up and it
Swirls and slushes in your bare hands.

I like it when it falls down like confetti in the air.

Keira Skillen (8)
Whittle-Le-Woods Primary School

Fluttering

Snow is white,
Snow is cold,
Everybody get inside,
Snow is as white as a piece of paper,
Ice is as hard as hard as a chair,
Snow is bumpy,
Snow is crunchy,
Snow is slippery,
Snow is soft,
Snow is very lovely.

Hannah Vickerman (8)
Whittle-Le-Woods Primary School

Build A Snowman

Let's make a snowman,
Start with body, roll, roll, and roll again,
Then the head, roll and roll,
I'm tired! Keep going,
Let's get a hat, a scarf and a pipe,
What about a coat?
Get some coal for his eyes,
Get a smiley stick for his mouth.
We are done!

Lily Dickinson (8)
Whittle-Le-Woods Primary School

A Whirling Whisk Of Snow

The snow is falling like snowdrops crumbling,
It's icy drops sprinkle on my nose,
The slush it leaves melts into your socks but not always,
Sometimes I walk out the door, it's crunchy
Like a dog, it's fluffy soft drops feel like a soft bed quilt.

Sarah Hanrahan (8)
Whittle-Le-Woods Primary School

Pets

(In remembrance of my Nana's dog, Sasha, the greatest dog ever)

I went to say goodbye,
Did you listen?

I saw you every Saturday,
Did you notice?

I saw you drive off with a sad expression on your face,
I knew what was happening, did you?

I felt the pain as the needle went in, as it pierced your skin.

I saw a tear trickle from your eye,
You were left there to die,
Goodbye old friend, goodbye.

Shannen Jo Lupton (10)
Whittle-Le-Woods Primary School

Winter Joys

White stars falling gently,
Softly down to Earth,
Red fires burning brightly,
In the warm and cosy hearth.

White trees changed elfin land
By red sun's dazzling glow,
Little Robin redbreasts.

Hopping in the snow.

Happy children's voices,
Shout loud with glee
Oh! The joys of winter,
Are wonderful to me.

Aneesh Bhadra (9)
Whittle-Le-Woods Primary School

The Greeks

The Greeks, the Greeks
How much they have to teach
About theatre, art and music
And how they wear their tunic
Oh the Greeks, the Greeks.

Oh the Greeks, the Greeks
How much they have to teach
Their famous myths and legends
With murder and with vengeance
The Greeks, the Greeks.

Oh the Greeks, the Greeks
How much they have to teach
Inventing the Olympic games
Bringing fun and fame
The Greeks, the Greeks.

Emily Toplis (10)
Whittle-Le-Woods Primary School

Sweets

Sugar sweets and lollipop treats
Toffee in the pot
A slimy face
What a wonderful place
The sticky treacle's hot

I go outside to the Robinson's tree
And guess what's out there waiting for me?
A basket full of chocolate and cake
I know my stay is not a mistake

But now the day is over
And I am beginning to feel sick
All those toffees and sweets I enjoyed
You can have them, take your pick!

Jennifer Litwinski (11)
Whittle-Le-Woods Primary School

Ghosts

They stretch,
They spin,
They float,
They have no skin,
The ghosts are coming.

They fly,
They scare,
They shout, 'Woooo!'
They don't have any hair,
The ghosts are coming.

They're scary,
They're frightening,
They're floaty,
They're as fast as lightning,
The ghosts are coming.

Grace Pulsford (10)
Whittle-Le-Woods Primary School

The Jungle

Rumble, rumble,
In the jungle,
Here the elephant comes,
Running away from the poachers' guns,
Run, run as fast as you can,
Here comes the mean man.

Rumble, rumble,
In the jungle,
Here the monkey comes,
Jumping around while he hums,
Jump, jump as high as you can,
Here comes the safari man.

Rachel Hull (10)
Whittle-Le-Woods Primary School

Haiku Poems

Planes

Flying through the air
Past everything that's alive
Nobody will see

Sea

Waves come towards me
No way forward, no way back
I stand alone now

Sun

Sun beaming downwards
Too hot to control for me
I am alone now

Rain

Rain striking the ground
No people out, nobody
I am alone now.

George Dobson (10)
Whittle-Le-Woods Primary School

The Roaring Volcano

The year is 3004
The volcano is alive
Rumble, rumble
Goes the volcano's tummy.
Steam's rising from his head
He's roaring to fire lava
The pressure's rising
Rocks popping and landing
Boom! Boom! Boom!
People terrified
The sound is immense.

Ryan Downs (10)
Whittle-Le-Woods Primary School

The Graveyard

It's old and crumbly,
Weird and mumbly,
Scary and rumbly,
Old and tumbly
The graveyard.

The dead live there,
You must beware,
The dead will scare,
The dark is there
The graveyard.

There's something near,
You cannot hear,
It's somewhere here,
It's something to fear
In the graveyard.

It's a vampire bat,
It's on your hat,
It's not a cat,
It will attack
In the graveyard.

This is no joke,
So don't hope,
It's no TV soap,
You've got to cope
In the graveyard.

You're coming out
Without a doubt,
So don't pout
Scream or shout
In the graveyard.

Do you like the graveyard?

Lucy Griffiths (10)
Whittle-Le-Woods Primary School

Treats

Gingerbread, toffee, chocolate and sweets,
Oh such lovely and wonderful treats.
Lollipops, candy, and liquorice too,
I'll bring some back just for you.

Jelly beans, jelly bears,
Dolly mix and chocolate eclairs.
You're in Heaven when you're here,
It's even better than Blackpool Pier!

Sugar laces, chocolate chips,
Caramel and strawberry lips.
Marshmallows and treacle are so sweet,
It is what we love to eat.

Chocolate balls and sugar mice,
Cherry cake - want a slice?
Jelly and ice cream, packets of sweets,
These are a child's favourite treats.

Now my trip is over, I'm starting to feel fat,
I waddle over to my car and there I have a chat.
My mother tells me, 'Come in - sit down!'
Oh no, oh no, I feel like a clown.

That night when I lie in bed,
I lie there still and rest my head.
Thinking of all the yummy treats,
Chocolate, laces, liquorice and sweets.

I wake up in the morning, remember all my dreams,
Sweets and candy and colourful streams,
I sit up and think,
I need a sweetie drink!

Oh such lovely sweets
Oh such wonderful treats.

Jessica Hall (10)
Whittle-Le-Woods Primary School

Night

Night is a being of strange beliefs,
He wears a hooded jacket covered in grease,
He moves on horseback and flies very low,
His eyes would be flame, he carries a bow,
His hair not of any woman or man,
He drinks only cola from a can,
When he drinks too much he turns in a mood,
He eats no man or thing, not even food,
He robs the rich and gives to the poor,
When he sees light he cries with a roar.

Thomas Robinson (10)
Whittle-Le-Woods Primary School

Winter Warmth

Trees that scoop the snow as it comes
The old man gathers his pearls like ice
As the snow twirls and whirls around him.

When he opens his very front door
The roaring fire fills the whole house
And the windows are flooded with snow.

As he settles down with a bubbling mug of cocoa
He watches the world drop asleep.

Sarah Knowles (10)
Whittle-Le-Woods Primary School

My Uncle's Dog

Every afternoon at three
My auntie comes to visit me
When we watch my uncle's dog
He runs round like a headless hog.

Then after he calms down
We take him for a walk in town.

Aaron Morris (10)
Whittle-Le-Woods Primary School

Colours

Orange, yellow, pink and green
How many colours have you seen?
I've seen lots, how about you?
My favourite colours are red and blue.
I love the sky because it's so blue,
I love the flowers any colour will do.
Grasses green, roses dark red
Brown is the colour of the wood on my bed.
In my dream colours are light
I go outside and fly my kite.
My kite is green,
How many colours have you seen.

Alexandra Rae Rimmer (11)
Whittle-Le-Woods Primary School

Winter

The trees sway in the whistling wind,
The cars skid on the icy road.
The children throwing snow at each other.
Inside the cat purring and sitting next to the fire.
The dogs barking loudly as their owners give them their food.

James McIver (10)
Whittle-Le-Woods Primary School

Winter

Winter is a slippery season
With biting snow, licking ice.
Shivering holes with itching rain
Flooding snow flowing through the heaven's door.

Jordan Heyworth (10)
Whittle-Le-Woods Primary School

School

I wake up in the morning at 7.30am,
I wash my face then I'm not dirty.
I have my breakfast a piece of toast,
I do my hair without a boast.
I kiss my mum before going to school,
And walk down the road and act all cool.
I catch the bus, I'm on my way,
I always pray there's no delay.
Alex is waiting at the gates,
Alex and me are very close mates.
Then we walk to the class,
And we all learn about capacity and mass.
Then we change our classes
Different passes.
I go to PE
She goes to ICT.

Lunchtime, here at last!

Sophie Smith (11)
Whittle-Le-Woods Primary School

Doggy Dog

Doggy dog, snug in bed
On a pillow place his head.
When he wakes, he yawns so loud
He walks to the street feeling proud.

Then he meets Mr Greaves
Walking round his stable knees.
Mr Greaves hands him a bone
Then he makes his way back home.

Doggy dog, snug in bed
On a pillow place his head.

James McGovern (11)
Whittle-Le-Woods Primary School

Seasons

All around the year there is lots of fun
The years enjoyed by everyone
Summer, spring, autumn and winter
Lots of treats from sweets to chocolate
The year just seems to fly by.

In spring there are lots to grow
Bright flowers beginning to show.

In summer there is brilliant sun
To make the children have their fun.

In autumn all the leaves do fall
But we still get to play football.

In winter some people do get snow
The birds pack their cases and go.

Bethan Swanwick (10)
Whittle-Le-Woods Primary School

Bonfire Night

Fire, fire burning bright,
In the darkness of the night.

Everyone, waiting quiet,
Nobody yet making a riot.

The firework is about to light,
We look up now, what a beautiful sight.

The colours, red and green and blue,
It's so nice, it couldn't be true.

Bonfire Night is so nice,
It can't be missed, even by mice.

Fire, fire burning bright,
In the darkness of the night.

Samuel Pattison (11)
Whittle-Le-Woods Primary School

Hay-Eater

One long tail,
Two big eyes
Hay-eater
Taking you for a ride
Wearing a bridle
What long legs
Lives in a stable
Galloping by.

Ashley Brown (10)
XII Apostles RC Primary School

Dog

Big, furry and fluffy,
A big, wet nose,
Four large paws,
Runs fast once going,
Bones and meat are favourites.
They are a favourites to people.
Would you love to have one?

Andrew Hodson (10)
XII Apostles RC Primary School

Snake

Slithers around
Fangs whiter than pearls
Long and slim
Devouring prey
Trails behind in the rain
Using tongue to know the way.

Louise McDonald (10)
XII Apostles RC Primary School

Mouse

Loves to nibble on everything
A long lashing tail
Whiskers which are long and grey
Small but very quiet
Creeping around at night
Eating people's left-overs.

Priscilla Devine (10)
XII Apostles RC Primary School

A Cat

Lies on the couch
Loves to play
Gets up early
Scary eyes
Sharp claws
Loves to kill.

Jonathan Sephton (11)
XII Apostles RC Primary School

Sly Snake

A swift animal,
Small but deadly
May be hard to see
Their teeth are knives
As poisonous as gas.

Thomas Rudd (11)
XII Apostles RC Primary School

Bird

Flies through the air
Lands anywhere
Drinks water, eats worms
Flies high, flies low
Flies anywhere
Swims fast, swims slow.

Ben Turner (11)
XII Apostles RC Primary School

Dog

Runs for a ball,
Sits waiting for food,
Barks at footsteps,
Taken out on a lead,
Bones for a snack,
Rips up slippers and then
Won't stop!

Nicole Fasoli (11)
XII Apostles RC Primary School

Miss Robinson Haiku

She has a great car
always got a smile on her
Laughing all thetime.

Kelly Causby (10)
XII Apostles RC Primary School

Sheep

Fluffy as a pillow,
Charges with its horns
Sounds so quiet
It's going with the rest
Comes in different colours
Lives on a mountain.

Naomi Green (11)
XII Apostles RC Primary School

Worm

Slithering through the tiniest gaps,
Has to dig through the soil,
Slippery as a bar of soap,
Slow as a slug,
Smoothly moves,
Eating disgusting things.

Thomas Spencer (10)
XII Apostles RC Primary School

Friends Haiku

Friends make me happy
Going shopping with my friends
Having lots of fun.

Margaret Unsworth (11)
XII Apostles RC Primary School

Leopard

A stealth-like creature
Runs like the wind
Never stops
Leaping, bounding and pouncing
Stalking, following and hunting
Never picky with food
Always take the opportunity to be the best.

Curtis Barnett (10)
XII Apostles RC Primary School

Horse

A chomping thing,
Grazing all day,
Eating green grass,
Trotting around the field,
Making loud noises,
Splashing in the mud,
Jumping over sticks.

Victoria Carney (11)
XII Apostles RC Primary School

Rugby Haiku

Running on the field
Kicking goals and scoring tries
Rugby is the sport.

Jonathan Ogden (11)
XII Apostles RC Primary School

Monkey

Swings from tree to tree,
Eats a lot of bananas,
Makes funny noises,
Makes a big mess,
Has a fluffy belly,
Jumps high to different branches,
Lands on the floor without getting hurt,
Plays in all of the autumn leaves,
Puts his hands under his arms and jumps,
Enjoys playing with humans.

Lauren Nicholas (10)
XII Apostles RC Primary School

The Eight-Legged Friend

Ready to pounce,
Calm and steady,
Eight-eyed concentration,
Webbing of the gods,
Silk finer than father's daughter,
Tunnels deeper than space itself,
Damp and hairy,
The eight-legged friend.

Aiden Slack (11)
XII Apostles RC Primary School